DISCARD

Selected Poems of P. K. Page

KALEIDOSCOPE

edited by Zailig Pollock

The Porcupine's Quill

Library and Archives Canada Cataloguing in Publication

Page, P. K. (Patricia Kathleen), 1916–2010
[Poems. Selections]
    Kaleidoscope : selected poems / P. K. Page; Zailig Pollock, editor.

(Collected works of P K Page ; v1)
ISBN 978-0-88984-331-8

    I. Pollock, Zailig.   II. Title.   III. Title: Poems. Selections.
IV. Series: Collected works of P K Page; v1

PS8531.A34A6 2010   C811'.54   C2010-903545-3

Published by The Porcupine's Quill, 68 Main Street, PO Box 160,
Erin, Ontario NOB 1T0. http://porcupinesquill.ca

Represented in Canada by the Literary Press Group.
Trade orders are available from University of Toronto Press.

We acknowledge the support of the Ontario Arts Council, the Canada Council for
the Arts, the Government of Canada through the Canada Book Fund and the
Ontario Media Development Corporation for our publishing programme.

A Note on the Collected Works of P. K. Page

Kaleidoscope: Selected Poems of P. K. Page is the first of a series of volumes being published by the Porcupine's Quill as a complement to the online hypermedia edition of the Collected Works of P.K. Page. The online edition is intended as a resource for scholarly research, while the print volumes are intended as attractive and inexpensive reading texts, edited to the highest scholarly standards but without the extensive textual apparatus which can be more effectively presented in a digital edition.

Introduction

1. Chinook

Randall Jarrell famously declared, 'A good poet is someone who manages, in a lifetime of standing out in thunderstorms, to be struck by lightning five or six times; a dozen or two dozen times and he is great.' Lists of P.K. Page's lightning strikes will differ from reader to reader – mine would include, at the very least, 'After Rain', 'Another Space', 'Arras', 'Beside You', 'Cry Ararat!', 'Deaf Mute in the Pear Tree', 'Evening Dance of the Grey Flies', 'Macumba: Brazil', 'My Chosen Landscape', 'The New Bicycle', 'Planet Earth', 'Presences', 'Stefan', 'The Stenographers', 'Photos of a Salt Mine', 'Stories of Snow' – but most readers would agree that few, if any, Canadian poets have been 'struck by lightning' more often than P.K. Page.

Page herself sometimes adopted Jarrell's metaphor:

> Hurl your giant thunderbolt that on my heart
> falls gently as a feather, falls and fills
> each crease and cranny of me…
>> ('Spinning')

but more frequently it is another metaphor that comes to her mind, the one which concludes the quatrain quoted above:

> – a chinook:
> sweet water, head to foot.

The chinook, the warm western wind whose sudden magical midwinter appearances Page often recalled from the Calgary of her childhood, is her muse. Like the 'gentle breeze' which Wordsworth invokes at the opening of his autobiographical *Prelude*, the chinook opens Page's own poetic autobiography, *Hand Luggage* (9):

> Calgary. The twenties. Cold and the sweet
> melt of chinooks. A musical weather.
> World rippling and running. World
> watery with flutes. And woodwinds.
> The wonder of water in that icy world.
> The magic of melt.

The spirit of the chinook returns at the end of *Hand Luggage* in the form of a recurrent dream: 'I dream of it often … the space where discreteness dissolves' (92). And in 'Another Space', a poem which literally began as a dream, she elaborates:

> It is as if a glass partition melts –
> or something I had always thought was glass –
> some pane that halved my heart
> is proved, in its melting, ice.

The invocation of the chinook in *Hand Luggage* is immediately followed by Page's description of herself as a 'borderland being'. Throughout her career, both as a poet and as a visual artist, Page remains fascinated with borders and their dissolution: the 'fluidity' of her poetry in which 'the self dissolves' (Sullivan 41–42) has its counterpart in the 'boundary play' of her visual art in which 'something shifts or merges' (Godard 65). Sometimes this dissolving and merging is explicitly linked with the chinook, as in the prose poem of that name, where the 'armour [of winter is] unlocked in a flash, its white flesh melted.' But even when the chinook is not explicitly named, the power of dissolution which it represents is repeatedly invoked. We sense this power when 'tightly locked [ice] dissolves, flows free' ('This Cold Man'); or 'glassy snow … melt[s]' ('Out Here: Flowering'); or 'dichotomy' becomes 'indivisible' ('Age of Ice'); or 'rigidity' that 'separates, divides' becomes 'molten' ('This Frieze of Birds'); or 'longitude that divides [and] that separates … dissolves' ('If It were You'); or 'walls dissolve' ('The Condemned'); or 'stiff[ness] … dissolve[s and] overflows' ('Probationer'); or 'visions … thaw […] and flow […]' ([Riel], P. K. Page fonds, 3–72: 12A). For Page 'the magic of melt' is so intimately connected with inspiration and creation that when she bids farewell to poetry, in what is probably the last poem she wrote before lapsing into her long mid-career silence, the chinook seems to be recalled by its absence:

Could I Write a Poem Now?

Or am I so
sold to the devil
that a hard frost locks
those lovely waters?

The hard frost that locked the lovely waters of Page's poetry in Brazil was to last until the very end of her years in Mexico when, in the central chinook moment of her career, with 'a sudden … bouleversement ('Questions and Images' 41) 'solid walls dissolved' ('Questions and Images' 40) and poetry soon began to flow again, as it would for the rest of her life.

The period of silence which 'Could I Write a Poem Now?' portends is the pivot around which Page's career turns. The poet who falls silent in Brazil and the one who finds her voice again in Mexico both created work of the highest order, but in vision and language the poetry of the earlier and of the later Page could hardly be more different. All readers of Page recognize this difference, but to explain its origin is a different matter.

The most illuminating accounts of the poetry of the early Page are provided by Brian Trehearne and Dean Irvine. Although their perspectives differ, both see Page's poetry of the forties and fifties as the product of a tension between opposing pairs of principles variously defined: personality and impersonality, interiority and exteriority, subjectivity and objectivity, multiplicity and wholeness. Trehearne emphasizes 'the aesthetic dimension of her crisis' (95). In his account Page is struggling with the legacy of the 'accumulative aesthetics' (92) of imagism, attempting to arrive at a 'new attitude to the relation between the individual image and the whole poem' (64). Irvine presents a gendered reading in which Page's struggle is between an 'objectivist, impersonalist … masculinist modernism' dominant in the Montreal milieu of the forties where she first found her voice, and a 'subjectivist, personalist … gender-conscious poetics' (130–31). And both convincingly argue that the tensions they identify in such masterful poems as 'The Stenographers', 'Photos of a Salt Mine', 'Stories of Snow', 'The Permanent Tourists', 'Arras', 'Giovanni and the Indians' and, especially, 'After Rain', eventually led to an impasse.

It is in 'After Rain' that this impasse is most powerfully dramatized. The speaker, clearly Page herself, describes the 'ruin' of her garden in a downpour, its 'geometry awash' in a kind of destructive version of the 'magic of melt' of the chinook. Paradoxically, she delights in this scene of destruction, which stimulates her imagination and unleashes a flood of vivid images. But her delight soon turns to 'shame' for reasons both of ethics and aesthetics. Her self-indulgent delight in the scene has blinded her to the 'ache' of the 'doleful' gardener whose work has been destroyed; and her similarly self-indulgent delight in evoking image after image – her 'whimsy' – has prevented her from creating a satisfying artistic whole. The poem ends with a prayer which clearly reflects her sense of being torn between the two warring aspects of her nature, the sensuousness that responds with great immediacy to the multiplicity and richness of art and nature, and the rationality that yearns for the 'meaning' provided by a larger 'whole':

> … keep my heart a size
> larger than seeing, unseduced by each
> bright glimpse of beauty striking like a bell,
> so that the whole may toll,
> its meaning shine
> clear of the myriad images that still –
> do what I will – encumber its pure line.

Although 'After Rain' provides us with a powerful dramatization of the tension between the opposing impulses at the heart of Page's poetry of the forties and fifties, in the end it leaves us 'no closer to the causes of Page's middle silence', to an understanding of why it is that 'pairs cannot be reconciled' (Trehearne 105, 45). The key to the 'enigma' of 'unsynthesized dialectical pairs' (Irvine 131, 132) is provided, in retrospect, by Page herself.

2.

> *Somewhere in between the two, a third*
> *wishes to speak, cannot make itself heard,*
> *stands unmoving, mute, invisible,*
> *a bolt of lightning in its naked hand.*
>   *– 'The Selves'*

In *Hand Luggage*, during a discussion of the destructive polarities of Canadian politics, Page recommends a 'Triclopian view' of the world:

> If only we could
> add an eye we would have a Triclopian view:
> … both of them, plus,
> … the two – with a third.

Seeing Page's career in the forties and fifties in terms of a conflict between pairs of opposites will take us only so far. It is only when we adopt a 'Triclopian view' and see the 'two – with a third' that we can hope to grasp the larger pattern of Page's loss of her poetic voice and its recovery during the period spanning her years in Brazil and Mexico. Page leaves us in no doubt as to the nature of the 'third,' when she describes the transformative moment that marks the end of her period of silence.

At the conclusion of the Mexico section of *Hand Luggage*, Page says of the years of fruitless struggle leading up to this moment:

> ... I had searched
> since birth, I suspect, via love, via art,
> via politics even – poor idiot me! –
> a magnet in search of its mother lode, or
> a chick for its hen? Incorrect, for a chick
> outgrows its necessity, mine had increased.
>
> I was starving, despairing, ...

But then

> ... onto my plate
> came, in typescript, my first introduction to Shah.
> Something in me was stilled. Some thirst was assuaged.

Shah is the Sufi master, Idries Shah, Page's guide through the world of the spirit, which was to be the still centre of her poetry in the years to come. Inspired by the Sufi vision 'of achieving a third perspective that emerges from an original dichotomy' (Stilles 203), Page is able to complement the opposing 'two' of her earlier work – the sensual and the rational – with a 'third' – the spiritual – which subsumes and fulfils them. Page's poetry thereafter abounds in visions of a oneness achieved through

> triangulation [which] enmesh[es]
> three worlds ...
> in timeless Time
> ('Flowers of the Upper Air')

Although visionary experiences of this sort find no expression in Page's poetry of the forties and fifties, it would be wrong to assume that they were entirely unknown to her when she first came to read Shah. As she tells us in 'Alphabetical' (and elsewhere, most notably in 'The First Part') such experiences were part of her childhood:

As a child I was wakened
taken from my tent
to look at the velvet
vastness of the night.

. . . . .

barefoot on the prairie
I looked deeper and deeper in.

Eternity rushed past.

But as time went on, she learned to

turn consciousness off
... no longer able to bear
so starry a totality
so vast a space ...

The very me of me gone ...

The extent to which Page struggled to 'turn consciousness off' can be seen in her most important work preceding her poetry of the forties, *The Sun and the Moon*, which she completed in 1940. At the core of this novella is the theme of the 'sweet ecstasy' of 'breath-taking communion' (7) repeatedly experienced by its protagonist Kristin. Kristin has the gift of 'empathy' (107) which enables her to enter into the being of whatever she perceives. But, to her horror, she learns that in entering into the being of Carl, the man she loves, she drains him, succubus-like, of his vitality. When Kirstin imagines this process, she envisions 'the slide of a glass in a phial which held two acids apart ... [being] destroyed by the acids and ultimately [bringing] them together to react' (119) – a kind of terrible parody of the melting of the glass partition in 'Another Space'. Her solution is to transfer her spirit into a tree and thus save Carl from being absorbed into the 'undivided mind'. The vision of spiritual wholeness, which Page would eventually come to celebrate, is here a source of 'terror' (119). At this stage of her life, Page has no way of making sense of it and there is nothing in her Canadian social or cultural milieu to help her.

Page's poetry of the forties and fifties, then, is marked not only by very real tensions between the two poles of the sensuous and the rational, but by the continued denial of the 'third' – the spiritual. It is when this denial becomes impossible to sustain ('I was starving') that Page falls silent; it is only when her spiritual hunger is finally 'assuaged' that her silence can be overcome.

3.

> *nel mezzo del camin*
> – *Dante*, Divine Comedy

The deeply moving drama of loss and recovery which reaches its dénouement at the precise chronological midpoint of Page's life, takes place in three countries, each of which has its unique role to play in the evolution of her 'Triclopian view'. Nothing had prepared Page for the life of an ambassador's wife that she was to embark on with her husband, Arthur Irwin; but, in retrospect, there seems to be an inevitability about her three-part physical and spiritual journey over these years.

Australia, the first stage of this journey, 'fascinated and appalled' Page, as a kind of distorted mirror in which she could view the Canada she had left behind. It was primarily the rational, critical side of Page's nature that Australia engaged, as she grappled with her place in a deeply conformist and self-satisfied society of 'ordinary people [who] understand ordinary things' ('Social Note'). It is in Australia that she produced some of her most intellectually challenging works – poems such as 'Arras', and 'After Rain' – in which she analyzes with great precision the increasing, and increasingly disturbing, gap between her art and the world around her.

But it was in Brazil that poetry finally became impossible for Page. The mostly fragmentary poems which survive from the period immediately leading up this crisis present us with the picture of a poet at a loss, unsure of what she has to say or how to say it:

> There should be more to say but I become
> when confronted – dumb –
> like a bird in a cage, can't sing on request
> ('There Should be More to Say', P.K. Page fonds, 27–5: 11)

In a curious reversal of the 'magic of melt' of wintry Calgary's chinook, tropical Brazil is imaged as 'green warm water dense / as a cube of green glass' ('The Heat and Weight of It', 27–5: 8) in which Page feels trapped and isolated. In another related image of isolation and entrapment, she sees the 'whole green world' of Brazil as a 'chrysoprase', a kind of precious green stone, 'crystal and spherical / silent as the hole in a head within'. At a loss for words, she sees only one possibility open to her: 'Paint it' ('This Whole Green World', 27–5: 4).

In Brazil, the poet P. K. Page becomes the painter P. K. Irwin, and, for a time, finds in this new art a release for the creative impulse that had been denied her as a poet. As we have seen, Trehearne identifies the central challenge which Page faced in the forties and fifties as 'the integration within a coherent "whole"' of an 'accumulation of brief images' (77, 61). In Brazil, this challenge continues to vex her as a poet: 'It is not enough to describe it / who wants a list?' ('There Should Be More to Say,' 27–5: 11) – but not as a painter. Freed of the demands of the intellect for a larger pattern of order and meaning, she begins to record, in drawing after drawing and in painting after painting, the images that 'pelt' her from every direction ('Questions and Images' 35). Page's joyous acceptance of the sensuous side of her nature is reflected in her diaries of the time. Compared to the Australian diaries, in the diaries of this period – and even more so in the *Brazilian Journal* based on them – there is little of the pungent social commentary that previously had so engaged her critical intellect.

There can be no doubt of the continuing, lifelong importance of the Brazilian years to Page. Cullen, her alter ego whose life journey she traced in a series of poems over a period of seventy years, ends his journey with a memory of Brazil. And, in her own life journey, the last work that Page completed was a version of a Brazilian fable. But although it is impossible to overestimate the importance of the Brazilian years, they were a passing phase. By the end of her time in Brazil, there is evidence both in her paintings, which are becoming more complex and disciplined, and in her diaries, that what Brazil has given her – permission to acknowledge and celebrate the sensuous aspect of her nature – is not enough. She writes 'there is a side of me which will always react to this place, a sensuous side … which loves all that loves the sun … but it is as if one dimension here is missing – the third, I think' (P.K. Page fonds, 113–16). Though she did not know it at the time, 'the third' was beckoning from Mexico.

'Black, black, black is the colour of a Mexican night' begins Page's Mexican diaries (133–26) establishing from the start that Mexico would be the site of 'the dark night of [her] soul' (*Hand Luggage* 81). The Mexican diaries are the record of an unbroken, and increasingly frantic, search for the spiritual sustenance that the sensuous richness of Brazil had been unable to offer her. Often on the edge of despair, Page seeks guidance from a wide variety of sources, including Jung, St. John of the Cross, C.S. Lewis, Gurdjieff, Subud (a spiritual movement originating in Indonesia), Zen, the 'perennial philosophy', and even – to the horror of Arthur

– Timothy Leary, who was visiting Mexico at the time. Deeply affected by the half-mad surrealist painter Leonora Carrington, during this period Page created her greatest paintings: for example, 'Cosmos' ('When Leonora saw it she said "I am having a heart attack"'), or 'And You, What do You Seek?' or 'The Garden' or 'The Dance'. These paintings make the stabs at surrealism in her poetry of the forties and fifties seem like child's play. Towards the end of the Mexican diaries, Page begins to refer to Idries Shah, but the diaries break off before her actual moment of discovery. It is only in her retrospective comments on this period, and in the poems which were to follow, that the impact of Shah, and of the Sufism to which he introduced her, fully registers.

Shah's version of Sufism, the central mystical tradition of Islam, is much contested by students of Islam, precisely because Shah denies its Islamic roots. He argues that Sufism is a universal mystical tradition which, for historical reasons, found a home in the Islamic world, but which has no deeper connection with Islam than with any other religious tradition. This, in itself, would have attracted Page, because she had no particular interest in Islam or in any other form of organized religion. More important, though, is the inclusive nature of Sufism. Sufism rejects all forms of dualism in favour of Page's 'Triclopic view' of a unified self consisting of *nafs* (sensation), *qalb* (understanding) and *ruh* (spirit). It is for this reason that the greatest spokesmen of Sufism are not philosophers and theologians, but poets. To the uninitiated, their verses can appear to be purely sensuous celebrations of love, wine, music and the beauties of the natural world; but to the understanding eye they embody spiritual truths. The spiritual discipline of Sufism, which Page took very seriously indeed, sanctioned her celebration of the sensuous world and provided her with an intellectual framework for this celebration.

4. *The Ice Age Is Over*

In 'Cry Ararat!', the first of many visionary poems inspired by Page's discovery of Sufism, the 'geometry awash' of 'After Rain' is countered by Mount Ararat 'emerging new-washed' from the Flood. 'Cry Ararat!' is the answer to the prayer in 'After Rain' for a vision of 'meaning' in 'the whole'. 'Something in me was stilled,' Page has told us, as a result of her encounter with Shah, and it is stillness which 'Cry Ararat!' celebrates. The vision of Mount Ararat is for those who 'do not reach to touch it / or labour to hear', who 'ask for nothing more / than stillness to receive'. But to receive this vision of the whole – 'the I-am animal, / the We-are leaf and flower' – one must be whole oneself, for 'this flora-fauna flotsam, pick and touch,

15

/ requires the focus of the total I.' In 'After Rain', the divided poet could do nothing to prevent 'the whole' from being overwhelmed by 'myriad images'. The closing lines of 'Cry Ararat!' acknowledge this danger – 'A single leaf can block a mountainside' – but they recognize the opposite possibility as well, that 'all Ararat [can] be conjured by a leaf.'

To characterize, in a few words, the diverse body of work that follows on 'Cry Ararat!' would be impossible, but there are certain qualities that stand out. Although relatively few of her poems allude specifically to Sufism ('Leather Jacket' is one exception), the series of visionary poems that begin with 'Cry Ararat!' (such as 'Another Space', 'Cosmologies', 'The Disguises', 'The End', 'The Flower Bed', 'Invisible Presences Fill the Air', 'Seraphim', 'Spinning' and 'The Yellow People in Metamorphosis') would be inconceivable without the stillness of spirit which Sufism enabled her to achieve. Even the most intellectually complex of these poems are characterized by the 'pure line' Page had prayed for in 'After Rain'. They tend to simple diction, free of the verbal knots and intricacies that had characterized most of Page's earlier verse. And along with these more visionary poems are numerous lyrics (such as 'Gift', 'Beside You', 'Stefan', The New Bicycle' and 'This Sky') of almost haiku-like directness, which register Page's unending delight in the world around her, a delight which, if anything, increases as she grows older. The simplicity of diction, vividness of imagery and lyric intensity of the later Page have made poems such as 'Planet Earth' much beloved beyond the usual circles of readers and students of poetry.

For a sense of the difference between late and early Page, one need only contrast the conclusions of 'Planet Earth' and 'Arras':

> It has to be made bright, the skin of this planet
> till it shines in the sun like gold leaf.
> Archangels then will attend to its metals
> and polish the rods of its rain.
> Seraphim will stop singing hosannas
> to shower it with blessings and blisses and praises
> and, newly in love,
> we must draw it and paint it
> our pencils and brushes and loving caresses
> *smoothing the holy surfaces.*
>   ('Planet Earth')

I thought their hands might hold me if I spoke.

> I dreamed the bite of fingers in my flesh,
> their poke smashed by an image, but they stand
> as if within a treacle, motionless,
> folding slow eyes on nothing.
>   While they stare
> another line has trolled the encircling air,
> another bird assumes its furled disguise.
>   ('Arras')

Not everyone will agree that 'Planet Earth' marks an advance over the much more challenging and cryptic 'Arras'. To some, as Trehearne puts it, Page 'may appear to have lowered the stakes of modernist form by adopting a more direct and colloquial imagery' (105). But whether we prefer the early Page or the late, it is clear that the 'focus of the total I' which first achieves poetic expression in 'Cry Ararat!' enables her to embark on a new phase of creativity, which was to continue unabated right up until her death in extreme old age, something that can be said of few other poets in history. One might be tempted to interpret the spiritual 'stillness' of the late Page as evidence of an inner retreat from the world, perfectly understandable in one her age; but this would be an error. If anything, the world is more present to her in her later years, for good or for ill, than it has ever been. Many of her later poems (such as 'Address at Simon Fraser' and 'Coal and Roses'), in which she vigorously decries the coarsening of contemporary consumer culture and the degradation of the natural environment, are more socially and politically engaged – and more convincingly so – than almost any of her earlier ones. And many (such as 'Suffering', 'A Grave Illness' and 'Masqueraders') record with a sharp and unsparing eye, though usually with self-deprecating wit and humour, the depredations of illness and old age. However, there is a great joy as well in her vivid sense of being in the world, a joy which, until the very end, continues to find its most powerful expression in her lifelong vision of magical renewal, 'the chinooks of [her] childhood' ('Green, How Much I Want You Green'):

> Come water, come springtime
> come my green lover
> with a whistle of grass
> to call me to clover.
> A key for my lock
> small flowers for my crown.
> The Ice Age is over,

green moss and green lichen

will paint a green lawn

that opens the road of dawn.

BIBLIOGRAPHY

Godard, Barbara. 'Kinds of Osmosis.' Catalogue for *Extraordinary Presence: The Worlds of P. K. Irwin*, Art Gallery of Peterborough, October 25–December 8, 2002. Rpt. *Journal of Canadian Studies* 38, 1 (Winter 2003): 65–75.

Irvine, Dean. *Editing Modernity. Women and Little-Magazine Cultures in Canada, 1916–1956*. University of Toronto Press, 2008.

Page, P. K. Page. P. K. Page fonds (MG30 D311/R2411), Library and Archives Canada.

—. *The Filled Pen: Selected Non-Fiction*. Ed. Zailig Pollock. University of Toronto Press, 2007.

—. *Hand Luggage: A Memoir in Verse*. The Porcupine's Quill, 2006.

—. *The Sun and the Moon and Other Fictions*. Ed. Margaret Atwood. Anansi, 1973.

Stiles, Dianne. '"The Person You Call 'I'": 'Configurations of Identity in the Poetry of P. K. Page.' Ph. D. dissertation, University of British Columbia, 2001.

Sullivan, Rosemary. 'A Size Larger Than Seeing: The Poetry of P. K. Page.' *Canadian Literature* 79 (1978): 32–42.

Trehearne, Brian. *The Montreal Forties: Modernist Poetry in Transition*. University of Toronto Press, 1999.

Textual Note

The date of composition is indicated after each poem. The poems are arranged in order of composition as it could be best determined from internal and external evidence; but the copy-texts used are the latest versions, for previously unpublished texts; and, for previously published texts, the latest published versions – with some exceptions. The exceptions involve some poems collected in *The Hidden Room* (1997). For poems from this collection which also occur in the later *Planet Earth* (2002) and *The Essential P.K. Page* (2008), it is the versions in *The Hidden Room* that have been used as copy-texts, since the later collections simply reprint these versions. However, sometimes (although not always), *The Hidden Room* uses versions of poems from the earliest collections in which they appear, rather than the latest, even when Page had revised the poems for later publication and had repeatedly authorized their reprinting over the years in the revised versions. Page herself either was unaware of this situation or did not fully appreciate its implications; and when I discussed the matter with her, she agreed to my suggestion that, in such cases, I should use the latest versions prior to *The Hidden Room* – from *The Glass Air* (1991). In addition, I have made minor changes to some of the texts in *The Hidden Room,* either because they contained typographical errors, which bedevil all editions, or because they had been altered from earlier versions in ways which seemed to indicate a misinterpretation of the textual situation. I made an effort to apprise Page of each of these instances and of my reasons for restoring the earlier readings, and her responses in every case were positive. However, she was not able to respond to my last batch of suggestions because they arrived too late – a few hours before her death. I have nevertheless incorporated these last emendations into the edition because I believe the case for them is compelling. For each of them I make the case in full in the online *Collected Works.*

In poems that extend over more than one page, the end of a sentence at the bottom of a page always coincides with the end of a stanza.

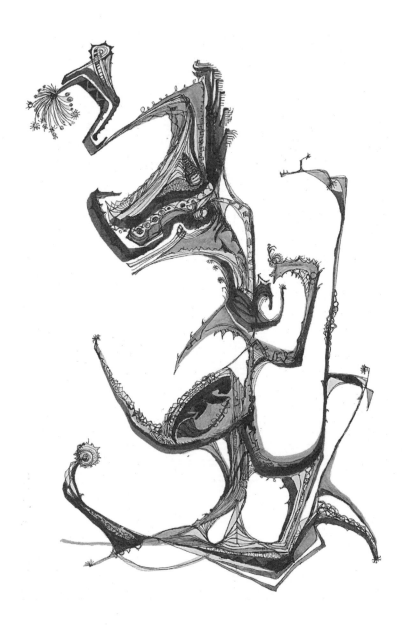

Ecce Homo

London had time to idle in galleries then.

We went together to the gallery in Leicester Square,
Epstein was showing there.
On the way you said
'Polygamy should be legalized … monogamy is dead.'
A wind of birds interrupted your words.
'Talking of birds,' you said,
'we tarred and feathered his Rima.
No … not I … but my race.
We are a queer people,
inarticulate and yet …
Ah! here is the place.'

We entered the gallery
but what I remember most
was my unexpected entry
into the door of my mind
with Rima as my host,
saying, as you had said,
'Monogamy is dead.'

People had never spoken like that before.
It had always been,
'Lovely weather we're having.'
Or, at the most,
'I wish I hadn't read
that awful book by Cronin, it's obscene.
Hatter's Castle it's called …
I shouldn't read it.'
Never dreaming a swift awakening was what I needed.

We entered the little room where *Ecce Homo* stood,
but it was bare to me.
I was away with Rima, discussing polygamy.
And then I felt your hand
tighten upon my arm
and heard you say in alarm,
'To understand,
Christ must be forgotten.
This is the mighty God. The God begotten
straight from the minds of the prophets,
straight from their fearful minds.
This is the God of plagues,
not the Christ who died
for love of humanity – the beautiful gentle Boy,
humorous, sunny-eyed.
Before you look,' you said,
'remember, remember it is not Christ,' you said.

I looked and the little room was filled with might,
with the might of fear in stone,
immense and shackled.
The flesh that covered the bone
seemed bone itself,
terrible, holy … you could not take a breath –
the Man, deformed, thick-hipped,
the God of Death,
in a little room in a gallery in Leicester Square,
silently standing there.

'There is much we do not know,'
you turned to me.
(Behold the Man, Rima, polygamy!)
'I think we should find somewhere nice and quiet for tea.
To think,' you said.
I nodded my head. 'To think,' I said.
And like a young tree I put out a timid shoot
and prayed for the day, the wonderful day when it bore its fruit.
And suddenly we were out in the air again.

London had time to idle in galleries then.

1941

Emergence

Come before rain;
rise like a dark blue whale
in the pale blue taffeta sea;
lie like a bar in the eyes where the sky should be.
Come before rain.

1941

The Crow

By the wave rising, by the wave breaking
high to low;
by the wave riding the air, sweeping the high air low
in a white foam, in a suds,
there
like a churchwarden, like a stiff
turn-the-eye-inward old man
in a cutaway, in the mist
stands
the crow.

1941

Desiring Only

Desiring only the lean sides of the stomach
sagging towards each other, unupholstered ...
pass me nothing of love done up in chocolates
or the fat first fruits of the tree
you planted from seed.

Desiring only the bone on the Mount of Venus
and the death rattle caught in the musical powder box ...
pass me no hand, then, as offertory,
no, nor sound of your voice.
Keep silent and do not touch me.
Even the air on my face is an effrontery.

Desiring only the bare soles of the feet
pacing triumphantly the ultimate basement ...
pass me no thick-carpeted personal contact,
nor little slippers of pity and understanding.

1942

The Mole

The mole goes down the slow dark personal passage –
a haberdasher's sample of wet velvet moving
on fine feet through an earth that only
the gardener and the excavator know.

The mole is a specialist and truly
opens his own doors; digs as he needs them
his tubular alleyways; and all his hills
are mountains left behind him.

1942

Cullen

Cullen renounced his cradle at fifteen,
set the thing rocking with his vanishing foot
hoping the artifice would lessen the shock.
His feet were tender as puffballs on the stones.

He explored the schools first and didn't understand
the factory-made goods they stuffed in his mind
or why the gramophone voice always ran down
before it reached the chorus of its song.
Corridors led 'from' but never 'to,'
stairs were merely an optical illusion,
in the damp basement where they hung their coats
he cried with anger and was called a coward.
He didn't understand why they were taught
life was good by faces that said it was not.
He discovered early 'the writing on the wall'
was dirty words scrawled in the shadowy hall.

Cullen wrote a note on his plate with the yolk of his egg
saying he hardly expected to come back,
and then, closing his textbooks quietly,
took his personal legs into the city.
Toured stores and saw the rats beneath the counters
(he visited the smartest shopping centres)
saw the worm's bald head rise in clerks' eyes
and metal lips spew out fantasies.
Heard the time clock's tune and the wage's pardon,
saw dust in the storeroom swimming towards the light
in the enormous empty store at night;
young heads fingering figures and floating freights
from hell to hell with no margin for mistakes.

Cullen bent his eye and paid a price
to sit on the mountain of seats like edelweiss –
watched the play pivot, discovered his escape
and with the final curtain went backstage;
found age and sorrow were an application,
beauty a mirage, fragrance fictionary,
the ball dress crumpled, sticky with grease and sweat.
He forgot to close the stage door as he went.

He ploughed the city, caught on a neon sign,
heard the noise of machines talking to pulp,
found the press treacherous as a mountain climb:
all upper case required an alpenstock.
Tried out the seasons then, found April cruel –
there had been no Eliot in his books at school –
discovered that stitch of knowledge on his own
remembering all the springs he had never known.
Summer grew foliage to hide the scar,
bore leaves that looked as light as tissue paper
leaves that weighed as heavy as a plate.
Fall played a flute and stuck it in his ear,
Christmas short-circuited and fired a tree
with lights and baubles; hid behind Christ; unseen
counted its presents on an adding-machine.

Cullen renounced the city, nor did he bother
to leave the door ajar for his return;
found his feet willing and strangely slipping like adders
away from the dreadful town.
Decided country, which he had never seen
was carillon greenness lying behind the eyes
and ringing the soft warm flesh behind the knees;
decided that country people were big and free.
Found himself lodgings with fishermen on a cliff,
slung his hammock from these beliefs and slept.

Morning caught his throat when he watched the men
return at dawn like silver-armoured Vikings
to women malleable as rising bread.
At last, the environment was to his liking.
Sea was his mirror and he saw himself
twisted as rope and fretted with the ripples;
concluded quietness would comb him out:
for once, the future managed to be simple.

He floated a day in stillness, felt the grass
grow in his arable body, felt the gulls
trace the tributaries of his heart and pass
over his river beds from feet to skull.
He settled with evening like a softening land
withdrew his chair from the sun the oil lamp made,
content to rest within his personal shade.
The women, gathering, tatted with their tongues
shrouds for their absent neighbours and the men
fired with lemon extract and bootlegged rum
suddenly grew immense.
No room could hold them – he was overrun,
trampled by giants, his grass was beaten down.
Nor could his hammock bear him, for it hung
limp from a single nail, salty as kelp.

Cullen evacuated overnight,
he knew no other region to explore;
discovered it was nineteen thirty-nine
and volunteered at once and went to war
wondering what on earth he was fighting for.
He knew there was a reason but couldn't find it
and marched to battle half an inch behind it.

1942

The Stenographers

After the brief bivouac of Sunday,
their eyes, in the forced march of Monday to Saturday,
hoist the white flag, flutter in the snow-storm of paper,
haul it down and crack in the mid-sun of temper.

In the pause between the first draft and the carbon
they glimpse the smooth hours when they were children –
the ride in the ice-cart, the ice-man's name,
the end of the route and the long walk home;

remember the sea where floats at high tide
were sea marrows growing on the scatter-green vine
or spools of grey toffee, or wasps' nests on water;
remember the sand and the leaves of the country.

Bell rings and they go and the voice draws their pencil
like a sled across snow; when its runners are frozen
rope snaps and the voice then is pulling no burden
but runs like a dog on the winter of paper.

Their climates are winter and summer – no wind
for the kites of their hearts – no wind for a flight;
a breeze at the most, to tumble them over
and leave them like rubbish – the boy-friends of blood.

In the inch of the noon as they move they are stagnant.
The terrible calm of the noon is their anguish;
the lip of the counter, the shapes of the straws
like icicles breaking their tongues, are invaders.

Their beds are their oceans – salt water of weeping
the waves that they know – the tide before sleep;
and fighting to drown they assemble their sheep
in columns and watch them leap desks for their fences
and stare at them with their own mirror-worn faces.

In the felt of the morning the calico-minded,
sufficiently starched, insert papers, hit keys,
efficient and sure as their adding machines;
yet they weep in the vault, they are taut as net curtains
stretched upon frames. In their eyes I have seen
the pin men of madness in marathon trim
race round the track of the stadium pupil.

1942

Personal Landscape

Where the bog ends, there, where the ground lips, lovely
is love, not lonely.
                              Land is
love, round with it, where the hand is;
wide with love, cleared scrubland, grain
on a coin.
Oh, the wheatfield, the rock-bound rubble;
the untouched hills
                              as a thigh smooth;
the meadow.
Not only the poor soil lovely, the outworn prairie,
but the green upspringing,
the lark-land,
the promontory.

A lung-born land,
a breath spilling,
scanned by the valvular heart's
field glasses.

1942

The Landlady

Through sepia air the boarders come and go,
impersonal as trains. Pass silently
the craving silence swallowing her speech;
click doors like shutters on her camera eye.

Because of her their lives become exact:
their entrances and exits are designed;
phone calls are cryptic. Oh, her ticklish ears
advance and fall back stunned.

Nothing is unprepared. They hold the walls
about them as they weep or laugh. Each face
is dialled to zero publicly. She peers
stippled with curious flesh;

pads on the patient landing like a pulse,
unlocks their keyholes with the wire of sight,
searches their rooms for clues when they are out,
pricks when they come home late.

Wonders when they are quiet, jumps when they move,
dreams that they dope or drink, trembles to know
the traffic of their brains, jaywalks their street
in clumsy shoes.

Yet knows them better than their closest friends:
their cupboards and the secrets of their drawers,
their books, their private mail, their photographs
are theirs and hers.

Knows when they wash, how frequently their clothes
go to the cleaners, what they like to eat,
their curvature of health, but even so
is not content.

And like a lover must know all, all, all.
Prays she may catch them unprepared at last
and palm the dreadful riddle of their skulls –
hoping the worst.

1943

As Ten As Twenty

For we can live now, love:
a million in us breathe,
moving as we move
and qualifying death

in lands our own and theirs
with simple hands as these
a walk as like as hers
and words as like as his.

They in us free our love
make archways of our mouths,
tear off the patent gloves
and atrophy our myths.

As ten, as twenty, now
we break from single thought
and rid of being two
receive them and walk out.

1943

Offices

Oh, believe me, I have known offices –
young and old in them, both –
morning and evening;
felt the air
stamp faces into a mould;
office workers at desks
saying *go* to a typewriter
and *stop* to a cabinet;
taking scrupulous care over calendars
so days
are etched in the outward-leaning eyes
while bosses, behind glass like jewels,
are flashing their light and coming suddenly near.

In offices drawers contain
coloured paper for copies,
staples, string,
hand lotion and various personal things
like love letters.

In washrooms girls are pretty with their mouths,
drawing them fancy; light the sugar-white tube of smoke
and never once question the future, look ahead
beyond payday or ask the *if* that makes them angular.

In elevators, coming and going, they are glib-
tongued and perky as birds with the elevator men.
Some, beautiful and coloured always, like singing,
never become the permanent collection
and some – if you speak to them of a different world,
a future more like life – become sharp,
give you their whittled face
and turn away like offended starlings from a wind.

1943

The Bands and the Beautiful Children

Band makes a tunnel of the open street
at first, hearing it;
seeing it band becomes
high: brasses ascending on the strings of sun
build their own auditorium of light,
windows from cornets
and a dome of drums.

And always attendant on bands, the beautiful children
white with running and innocence;
and the arthritic old
who, patient behind their windows
are no longer split by the quick yellow of imagination
or carried beyond their angular limits of distance.

But the children move
in the trembling building of sound,
sure as a choir
until band breaks and scatters,
crumbles about them and is made of men
tired and grumbling
on the straggling grass.

And the children, lost, lost,
in an open space,
remember the certainty of the anchored home
and cry on the unknown edge of their own city
their lips stiff from an imaginary trumpet.

1944

Element

Feeling my face has the terrible shine of fish
caught and swung on a line under the sun
I am frightened held in the light that people make
and sink in darkness freed and whole again
as fish returned by dream into the stream.

Oh running water is not rough; ruffled to eye,
to flesh it is flat and smooth; to fish
silken as children's hands in milk.

I am not wishful in this dream of immersion.
Mouth becomes full with darkness
and the shine, mottled and pastel, sounds its own note, not
the fake high treble thrown on resounding faces.

There are flowers – and this is pretty for the summer –
light on the bed of darkness;
there are stones that glisten and grow slime;
winters that question nothing, are a new
night for the passing movement of fine fins;
and quietly, by the reeds or water fronds
something can cry without discovery.

Ah in daylight the shine is single
as dime flipped or gull on fire or fish
silently hurt – its mouth alive with metal.

1944

Stories of Snow

Those in the vegetable rain retain
an area behind their sprouting eyes
held soft and rounded with the dream of snow
precious and reminiscent as those globes –
souvenir of some never-nether land –
which hold their snow-storms circular, complete,
high in a tall and teakwood cabinet.

In countries where the leaves are large as hands
where flowers protrude their fleshy chins
and call their colours,
an imaginary snow-storm sometimes falls
among the lilies.
And in the early morning one will waken
to think the glowing linen of his pillow
a northern drift, will find himself mistaken
and lie back weeping.
And there the story shifts from head to head,
of how in Holland, from their feather beds
hunters arise and part the flakes and go
forth to the frozen lakes in search of swans –
the snow-light falling white along their guns,
their breath in plumes.
While tethered in the wind like sleeping gulls
ice-boats wait the raising of their wings
to skim the electric ice at such a speed
they leap jet strips of naked water,
and how these flying, sailing hunters feel
air in their mouths as terrible as ether.
And on the story runs that even drinks
in that white landscape dare to be no colour;
how flasked and water clear, the liquor slips

silver against the hunters' moving hips.
And of the swan in death these dreamers tell
of its last flight and how it falls, a plummet,
pierced by the freezing bullet
and how three feathers, loosened by the shot,
descend like snow upon it.
While hunters plunge their fingers in its down
deep as a drift, and dive their hands
up to the neck of the wrist
in that warm metamorphosis of snow
as gentle as the sort that woodsmen know
who, lost in the white circle, fall at last
and dream their way to death.

And stories of this kind are often told
in countries where great flowers bar the roads
with reds and blues which seal the route to snow –
as if, in telling, raconteurs unlock
the colour with its complement and go
through to the area behind the eyes
where silent, unrefractive whiteness lies.

1944

Adolescence

In love they wore themselves in a green embrace.
A silken rain fell through the spring upon them.
In the park she fed the swans and he
whittled nervously with his strange hands.
And white was mixed with all their colours
as if they drew it from the flowering trees.

At night his two-finger whistle brought her down
the waterfall stairs to his shy smile
which, like an eddy, turned her round and round
lazily and slowly so her will
was nowhere – as in dreams things are and aren't.

Strolling along avenues in the dark
street lamps sang like sopranos in their heads
with a violence they never understood
and all their movements when they were together
had no conclusion.

Only leaning into the question had they motion;
after they parted were savage and swift as gulls.
Asking and asking the hostile emptiness
they were as sharp as partly sculptured stone
and all who watched, forgetting, were amazed
to see them form and fade before their eyes.

1945

Election Day

I

I shut the careful door of my room and leave
letters, photographs and the growing poem –
the locked zone of my tight and personal thought
slough off – recede from down the green of the street.
Naked almost among the trees and wet –
a strike for lightning.

And everything rushes at me either fierce or friendly
in a sudden world of bulls.
Faces on posters in the leaves call out
the violent yes or no to my belief.
Are quick or slow or halted to my pulse.

Oh on this beautiful day, the weather wooing
the senses and the feel of walking
smooth in my summer legs
I lope through the tall and trembling grass and call
the streaming banner of my public colour.

II

Here in this place, the box and private privet
denote the gentleman and shut him in –
for feudally he lives and the feud on.
Colonel Evensby with his narrow feet
will cast his blue blood ballot for the Tory.

And in the polling station I shall meet
the smiling rather gentle overlords
propped by their dames and almost twins in tweeds
and mark my x against them and observe
my ballot slip, a bounder, in the box.

And take my route again through lazy streets
alive with all-out blossoming, through trees
that stint no colour for their early summer
and past an empty lot where an old dog
appoints himself as guardian of the green.

III

Radio owns my room as the day ends.
The slow returns begin, the voices call
the yes's and the no's that ring or toll;
the districts all proclaim themselves in turn
and public is my room, not personal.

Midnight. I wander on the quiet street,
its green swamped by the dark; a pale glow
sifts from the distant lamps. Behind the leaves
the faces on the posters wait and blow
tattered a little and less urgent now.

I pass the empty lot. The old dog
has trotted off to bed. The neighbourhood
is neatly hedged with privet still, the lights
are blinking off in the enormous homes.
Gentlemen, for the moment, you may sleep.

1945

If It Were You

If it were you, say, you
who scanning the personal map one day knew
your sharp eyes water and grow colour blind,
unable to distinguish green from blue
and everything terribly run together as if rain
had smudged the markings on the paper –
a child's painting after a storm –
and the broad avenue erased,
the landmarks gone;
and you, bewildered – not me this time and not
the cold unfriendly neighbour or the face in the news –
who walked a blind circle in a personal place;

and if you became lost, say, on the lawn,
unable to distinguish left from right
and that strange longitude that divides the body
sharply in half – that line that separates
so that one hand could never be the other –
dissolved and both your hands were one,
then in the garden though birds went on with their singing
and on the ground
flowers wrote their signatures in coloured ink –
would you call help like a woman assaulted,
cry to be found?

No ears would understand. Your friends and you
would be practically strangers, there would be no face
more familiar than this unfamiliar place
and there would be walls of air, invisible, holding
you single and directionless in space.

First you would be busy as a woodsman marking
the route out, making false starts and then
remembering yesterday when it was easy

you would grow lazy.
Summer would sit upon you then as on a stone
and you would be tense for a time beneath the morning sun
but always lonely
and birds perhaps would brush your coat and become
angels of deliverance
for a moment only;
clutching their promising wings you would discover
they were illusive and gone
as the lost lover.
Would you call Ariel, Ariel, in the garden,
in a dream within a dream be Orpheus
and for a certain minute take a step
delicately across the grass?

If so, there would be no answer nor reply
and not one coming forward from the leaves.
No bird nor beast with a challenging look
or friendly.
Simply nothing but you and the green garden,
you and the garden.

And there you might stay forever, mechanically
occupied, but if you raised your head
madness would rush at you from the shrubbery
or the great sun, stampeding through the sky
would stop and drop –
a football in your hands –
and shrink as you watched it
to a small dark dot
forever escaping focus
like the injury to the cornea which darts
hard as a cinder across the sight but dims
fading into the air like a hocus-pocus
the minute that you are aware
and stare at it.

Might you not, if it were you,
bewildered, broken,
slash your own wrists, commit
an untidy murder in the leafy lane
and scar the delicate air with your cries or sit
weeping, weeping in the public square
your flimsy butterfly fingers in your hair
your face destroyed by rain?

If it were you, the person you call 'I',
the one you loved and worked for,
the most high
now become Ishmael,
might you not
grow phobias about calendars and clocks,
stare at your face in the mirror, not knowing it
and feel an identity with idiots and dogs
as all the exquisite unborns of your dreams
deserted you to snigger behind their hands?

1945

Round Trip

The passenger boards the waiting train –
he is white
and poised as the sculptured gull in flight;
his matching bags might be packed with air –
they are neat and flat.
Now he removes his hat,
smooths back his hair,
arranges his long pressed legs away from the aisle.
(The girl inside, meanwhile,
afraid of adventure,
trembles against his wrought-iron ribs like paper.)
He waves through the window a last farewell,
his pale
sigh of a hand caressing the delicate pane
blots out the faces one by one as though
he were snuffing candle flames.

All is prepared for the incredible journey:
in the baggage car his trunks contain a sword,
binoculars and compass, powdered food,
shorts and a solar topee for the south,
letters of introduction and a mask.
A lifetime lies behind him
he has left
the tightly frozen rivers of his blood
the plateaux of his boredom
and the bare
buttonholes his pallid eyes had cut.

Ahead – perhaps the mountains and the hot
colours of the tropics
and the sun
awaiting only his miraculous foot.

Settled, he sighs. The train devours its track
(the girl cries for her mother),
he is hot,
adjusts the air conditioner,
dares not
shed his respectable beginner's coat
fearing the ill-drawn map it might uncover.
Suffers unspeaking,
neither nods nor smiles
to anyone nearby.
Decides the country he is passing through
may offer some escape,
straightens his tie
and contemplates the view.

Unveiling the sluggish eye that is drugged with future
he notes the place where the sienna soil
makes an incision in the field of mustard
clotted against the acid drops of the poplars;
dilates the pupil's I as he approaches
the perpetual great-god-green upending marshes
where grey and ageing barns with a family likeness
are scattered about like relatives in a village.
A bridge against the sky,
with metal girders
that droop in long black leaves,
forms a grove of palms –
a hot illusion set with circling birds.

But 'like' or 'as' is not what he is searching.
Something is hidden in the scenery still –
the hero hovers just behind the curtain
articulating the perfect unheard words
and the changing country is only a view that swings
the silent globes of the eyes but nothing more,
for his eyes, unlike a doll's, have no lead ball
attached behind the nose to rise and fall.

A white house, stark with the memory of home,
jumps from the unseen field – an ace in his face –
and slips back swiftly in the indolent pack.
(He feels the girl's long-fingered hands like tears,
feels the contortions of her weeping face.)
And his mind in a tantrum draws its filmy shutter
invisibly across the dot of sight
turning the country into the negative, no
country of faint or fit.
Trees pass and pass,
the quick rush of their noise
the Niagara of blood evacuating the head,
while passengers in a trance of boredom or bright
with the coloured excitement of a child in fever
move along the corridors of plush
as if they had no choice.
A surgeon's voice pierces his deafened ears:
'Trains don't take you anywhere, nor cars –
they're just another standstill thing on wheels
screaming at full-speed stop through the moving landscape
and returning you to yourself –
it's a boomerang business
with the pretty revolving set of the old-time movies.'

> The traveller sleeps,
> in dreams explores the place
> where everything is foreign:

the orange groves and the quick
walk of the women
which fit together like glass arithmetic.
The sheen that lies on gutters in gold leaf.
(The dream of falling followed him, he fell
sideways along sierras
down through boughs
where monkeys smiled at him with his own mouth.)
But everyone recognized him for their own.
In such sweet rain his ears and armpits grew
flowers and hummingbirds were part of him –
hanging jewels upon lapel and hat.
At night the oranges and lemons cut
small amber caves from darkness where he sat
and the mercurial rivers found their seas
at any spot he bathed.
When storms came up, fish glanced the thickened air.
Nothing was permanent and everywhere
immediate as music, slick as silk.
With daylight silver girls on silver stilts
called in his turret window as he woke.
(But still the dream of falling followed him:
he fell through bubble faces, fell through trees,
he fell through purple fulminating smoke,
through hands that were only gloves and arms that were sleeves.)
Then falling passed and everywhere he looked
was bright, for diamonds had replaced his eyes.

Awake he sees the baking soil, the cracked
packets of earth
where thin anaemic weeds are grass snakes.
Following that, the desert:
sand seeps between the badly fitting windows,
clings to his teeth,

settles beneath his nails.
Later he feels it pumping through his heart –
a mechanical hourglass.
Invisible as lice it crawls and spreads
over the sheets, the pillow's stuffed with it
and all night long it roars in his ears,
sifts over him as if it is wanted and loved,
settles in crease and pore; is his.
To be caught in a glacier, he thinks, to be mint
in the heart of an ice cube,
to be contained in anything smooth, to touch
a hardwood floor in Iceland.
(The girl inside, with a rosary of sand
repeats her Aves and the Paternoster.)
He dozes fitfully and dreams he wakes,
wakes, thinks he's dreaming, tries to break his dreams,
feels feverish, attempts to take his pulse.

Light settles on his face at last in mist,
raising the blind the world is mist forever
and focus has to shift and shift for far
and near are now identical –
colourless, shapeless – echoing ghosts of snow.
Oh, where is what he dreamed, forever where
the landscape for his pattern? The desired
and legendary country he had planned?
In all this mist, he says, in all this mist,
a man might not exist,
a man might be
an empty snakeskin.

And as he thinks, the train is losing speed,
behaves as if the mist had clogged its wheels,
becomes a caterpillar mired in glue
                                and stops.
'Home Town,' the porter calls. 'End of the track.'
And all the passengers, as if they knew,
and undeceived by fantasy or folder,
descend the waiting steps
and vanish in the mist
which hides the station and obstructs the view.

The traveller is lost. (His crying girl
grown into empress
moans, 'Betrayed! Betrayed!')
He blocks his ears to her,
smooths back his hair,
prepares for the adventure with a smile,
swings to the door with an explorer's stride
and steps upon the platform to be met
by everyone he left.
Their waving hands are little flags for him
fluttering and blowing. Coming near
he hears the words their moving mouths repeat:
that nothing's changed, that everything's the same.
And though he cannot see because of mist
he knows it's true – that everything's the same.

Forever, everywhere, for him, the same.

1945

This Cold Man

Now this cold man in his garden feels the ice
thawing from branches of his lungs and brain;
the blood thins out in artery and vein,
the stiff eyes slip again.

Kneeling in welters of narcissus his
dry creaking joints bend with a dancer's ease,
the roughened skin softens beneath the rain

and all that he had clutched, held tightly locked
behind the fossil frame
dissolves, flows free
in saffron covering the willow tree
and coloured rivers of the rockery.

Yellow and white and purple is his breath,
his hands are curved and cool for cupping petals,
the sharp green shoots emerging from the beds
all whistle for him

until he is the garden – heart the sun
and all his body soil;
glistening jonquils blossom from his skull,
the bright expanse of lawn his stretching thighs
and something rare and perfect, yet unknown,
stirs like a foetus just behind his eyes.

1945

Only Child

The early conflict made him pale
and when he woke from those long weeping slumbers she was there
and the air about them – hers and his –
sometimes a comfort to him, like a quilt, but more
often than not a fear.

There were times he went away – he knew not where –
over the fields or scuffing to the shore;
suffered her eagerness on his return
for news of him – where had he been, what done?
He hardly knew, nor did he wish to know
or think about it vocally or share
his private world with her.

Then they would plan another walk, a long
adventure in the country, for her sake –
in search of birds. Perhaps they'd find the blue
heron today, for sure the kittiwake.

Birds were familiar to him now, he knew
them by their feathers and a shyness like his own
soft in the silence.
Of the ducks she said, 'Observe,
the canvas-back's a diver,' and her words
stuccoed the slaty water of the lake.

He had no wish to separate them in groups
or learn the latin,
or, waking early to their song remark, 'The thrush,'
or say at evening when the air is streaked
with certain swerving flying,
'Ah, the swifts.'

Birds were his element like air and not
her words for them – making them statues
setting them apart,
nor were they facts and details like a book.
When she said, 'Look!'
he let his eyeballs harden
and when two came and nested in the garden
he felt their softness, gentle, near his heart.

She gave him pictures which he avoided, showing
strange species flat against a foreign land.
Rather would he lie in the grass, the deep grass of the island
close to the gulls' nests knowing
these things he loved and needed near his hand,
untouched and hardly seen but deeply understood.
Or sail among them through a wet wind feeling
their wings within his blood.

Like every mother's boy he loved and hated
smudging the future photograph she had,
yet struggled within the frames of her eyes and then
froze for her, the noted naturalist –
her very affectionate and famous son.
But when most surely in her grasp, his smile
darting and enfolding her, his words:
'Without my mother's help ...' the dream occurred.

Dozens of flying things surrounded him
on a green terrace in the sun
and one by one
as if he held caresses in his palm
he caught them all and snapped and wrung their necks
brittle as little sticks.
Then through the bald, unfeathered air
and coldly as a man would walk
against a metal backdrop, he
bore down on her
and placed them in her wide maternal lap
and accurately said their names aloud:
woodpecker, sparrow, meadowlark, nuthatch.

1945

Outcasts

Subjects of bawdy jokes and by the police
treated as criminals, these lovers dwell
deep in their steep albino love –
a tropic area where nothing grows.

Nobody's brothers, they revolve
on rims of the family circle, seek some place
where nothing shuns them, where no face
in greeting dons the starched immaculate mask.

Look, in their isolation they become
almost devoid of bones, their ward is one
nobody enters, but their least
window requires a curtain. They are clowns

without a private dressing room, with only
one ancient joke to crack now and forever.
They draw a crowd as if they had a band:
Always the healthy are their audiences.

The youths who hunt in packs, bitches with cash,
crafty embezzlers of the public purse,
perjurers and fashionable quacks
slumming, but saintly, saintly, judge them as

outcasts. In the laundered mind they rate
the bottom of the scale, below the Jew
with his hundred hands and pockets and below
niggers whose love is lewd.

Let doctors show a white aseptic hand
within their sickroom and let parents gaze
back against time's tight fist to find the cause –
seek in the child the answer to the man:

search out the early misfit, who at school,
sickly for love and giddy with his sex
found friendship like a door banged in his face,
his world a wasteland and himself a fool.

1946

Puppets

See them joined by strings to history:
their strange progenitors all born full-grown,
ancestors buried with the ancient Greeks –
slim terra-cotta dolls with articulate limbs
lying like corpses.
                    Puppets in Rome
subject to papal law, discreet in tights.

And see the types perpetuate themselves
freed from the picket prejudice of race:
the seaside Punch with his inherited nose
carried from Pulcinella round the globe
ends up in Bexhill, enters English eyes.

While here in a Sunday drawing-room beside
the bland Pacific and its rain come two
emerging full-grown from their dark cocoons –
two whose blasé antecedents once
performed for Pepys's mistress, or, in silk,
were bawdy for bored royalty at court;
escaped and raided country fairs and spread
the world with areas of Lilliput.

Before our eyes the twelve-inch clown grows large
and dances on his rubber feet and kicks
pneumatic legs, thumbs his enormous nose;
lies down for push-ups – and, exhibitionist –
suddenly turns and waves.
More clown than clowns he is all laughter, is
buoyed by it and brilliant in its light.
Unlike his living prototype has no
dichotomy to split him: this is all.
He calls your laughter out without reserve –
is only and always feet and a vulgar streak
and his music, brass.

The negro does a tap dance and his toes
click on the parquet.
Music moves in him and explodes in his toes
and somehow he is two-fold, though he grins
his hands are stripped of humour,
they are long
and lonely attached to him.
He is himself and his own symbol,
sings
terribly without a voice, is so
gentle it seems that his six delicate strings
are ropes upon him.
But still he grins, he grins.

Oh, coming isolated from their plays but not
isolated from their history,
shaped and moulded by heredity,
negro and clown in microcosm, these
small violent people shake the quiet room
and bring all history tumbling about
a giant audience that almost weeps.

1946

Young Girls

Nothing, not even fear of punishment
can stop the giggle in a girl.
Oh mothers' trim
shapes on the chesterfield cannot dispel
their lolloping fatness.
Adolescence tumbles about in them
on cinder schoolyard or behind the expensive gates.

See them in class like porpoises
with smiles and tears
loosed from the same subterranean faucet; some
find individual adventure in
the obtuse angle, some in a phrase
that leaps like a smaller fish from a sea of words.
But most, deep in their daze, dawdle and roll,
their little breasts like wounds beneath their clothes.

A shoal of them in a room makes it a pool.
How can one teacher keep the water out,
or, being adult, find the springs and taps
of their tempers and tortures?
Who on a field filled with their female cries
can reel them in on a line of words
or land them neatly in a net?
On the dry ground they goggle, flounder, flap.

Too much weeping in them and unfamiliar blood
has set them perilously afloat.
Not divers these – but as if the waters rose in flood –
making them partially amphibious
and always drowning a little and hearing bells;
until the day the shore line wavers less,
and caught and swung on the bright hooks of their sex,
earth becomes home, their natural element.

1946

Man with One Small Hand

One hand is smaller than the other. It
must always be loved a little like a child;
requires attention constantly, implies
it needs his frequent glance to nurture it.

He holds it sometimes with the larger one
as adults lead a child across the street.
Finding it his or suddenly alien
rallies his interest and his sympathy.

Sometimes you come upon him unawares
just quietly staring at it where it lies
as mute and somehow perfect as a flower.

But no. It is not perfect. He admits
it has its faults: it is not strong or quick.
At night it vanishes to reappear
in dreams full-size, lost or surrealist.

Yet has its place like memory or a dog –
is never completely out of mind – a rod
to measure all uncertainties against.

Perhaps he loves it too much, sets too much stock
simply in its existence. Ah, but look!
It has its magic. See how it will fit
so sweetly, sweetly in the infant's glove.

1947

Paranoid

He loved himself too much. As a child was god.
Thunder stemmed from his whims,
flowers were his path.
Throughout those early days his mother was all love,
a warm projection of him
like a second heart.

In adolescence, dark and silent, he was perfect;
still godlike and like a god
cast the world out.
Crouching in his own torso as in a chapel
the stained glass of his blood
glowed in the light.

Remained a god. Each year he grew more holy
and more wholly himself.
The self spun
thinner and thinner like a moon forming
slowly from that other self
the dead sun.

Until he was alone, revolved in ether
light years from the world,
cold and remote.
Thinking he owned the heavens too, he circled,
wanly he turned and whirled
reflecting light.

1948

The Permanent Tourists

Somnolent through landscapes and by trees
nondescript, almost anonymous,
they alter as they enter foreign cities –
the terrible tourists with their empty eyes
longing to be filled with monuments.

Verge upon statues in the public squares
remembering the promise of memorials
yet never enter the entire event
as dogs, abroad in any kind of weather,
move perfectly within their rainy climate.

Lock themselves into snapshots on the steps
of monolithic bronze as if suspecting
the subtle mourning of the photograph
might later conjure in the memory
all they are now incapable of feeling.

And search all heroes out: the boy who gave
his life to save a town; the stolid queen;
forgotten politicians minus names
and the plunging war dead, permanently brave,
forever and ever going down to death.

Look, you can see them nude in any café
reading their histories from the bill of fare,
creating futures from a foreign teacup.
Philosophies like ferns bloom from the fable
that travel is broadening at the café table.

Yet somehow beautiful, they stamp the plaza.
Classic in their anxiety they call
all sculptured immemorial stone
into their passive eyes, as rivers
draw ruined columns to their placid glass.

1948

Portrait of Marina

Far out the sea has never moved. It is
Prussian forever, rough as teaselled wool
some antique skipper worked into a frame
to bear his lost four-master.
                              Where it hangs
now in a sunny parlour, none recalls
how all his stitches, interspersed with oaths
had made his one pale spinster daughter grow
transparent with migraines – and how his call
fretted her more than waves.
                              Her name
Marina, for his youthful wish –
boomed at the font of that small salty church
where sailors lurched like drunkards, would, he felt
make her a water woman, rich with bells.
To her, the name Marina simply meant
he held his furious needle for her thin
fingers to thread again with more blue wool
to sew the ocean of his memory.
Now, where the picture hangs, a dimity
young inland housewife with inherited
clocks under bells and ostrich eggs on shelves
pours amber tea in small rice china cups
and reconstructs
how great-great-grandpappa at ninety-three
his fingers knotted with arthritis, his
old eyes grown agaty with cataracts
became as docile as a child again –
that fearful salty man –
and sat, wrapped round in faded paisley shawls
gently embroidering.
While Aunt Marina in grey worsted, warped
without a smack of salt, came to his call
the sole survivor of his last shipwreck.

*

Slightly offshore, it glints. Each wave is capped
with broken mirrors. Like Marina's head
the glinting of these waves.
She walked forever antlered with migraines
her pain forever putting forth new shoots
until her strange unlovely head became
a kind of candelabra – delicate –
where all her tears were perilously hung
and caught the light as waves that catch the sun.
The salt upon the panes, the grains of sand
that crunched beneath her heel
her father's voice, 'Marina!' – all these broke
her trembling edifice. The needle shook
like ice between her fingers.
In her head
too many mirrors dizzied her and broke.

*

But where the wave breaks, where it rises green
turns into gelatine, becomes a glass
simply for seeing stones through, runs across
the coloured shells and pebbles of the shore
and makes an aspic of them
then sucks back
in foam and undertow –
this aspect of the sea
Marina never knew.

For her the sea was Father's Fearful Sea
harsh with sea serpents
winds and drowning men.
For her it held no spiral of a shell
for her descent to dreams,
it held no bells.
And where it moved in shallows it was more
imminently a danger, more alive
than where it lay offshore full fathom five.

1949

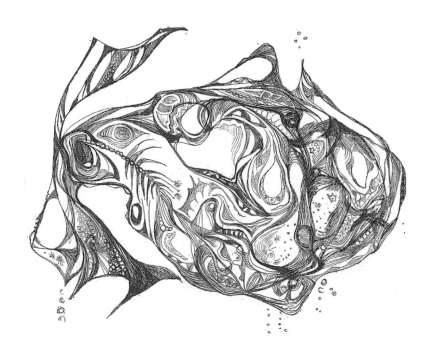

Reflection in a Train Window

There is a woman floating in a window –
transparent –
Christmas wreaths in passing houses
shine now in eye and now in hair, in heart.
How like a saint with visions, the stigmata
marking her like a martyr.

Merged with a background of mosaic
she drifts
through tenement transoms, independent stars,
while in between her and herself the sharp
frost crystals prick the pane with thorns.

She without substance, ectoplasmic, still,
is haloed with the reading lamps of strangers
while brass and brick pass through her.
                                    Yet she stirs
to some soft soundless grieving and tears well
in her unseeing eyes and from the sill
her trembling image falls, rises and falls.

c. 1949–50

Giants

It is not the same, only bigger, being a giant.

At first, they say, you hardly notice it
but experience teaches quickly and you learn
various differences.
It is worse to lie, for instance, when the world
hears every word you say.
And the habit of thinking more and speaking less
grows on you early in life as a result.
Some people think that giants are mute.
They're not.

Some people think they are saints. It isn't true.
It's easy enough to dispense with comfort when
nothing is comfortable.
Property isn't a goal when it doesn't fit.

And I've often heard it said they have no heart.
They say themselves, their tears would flood the world
if once they let things move them. As it is
they quickly learn soft-heartedness is cruel.

But it's when they age that things get really tough.
As soon as irregularities occur
they have to be on their guard.
Consider a giant's myopia – the vague
mist of his gaze
shrouding the world with gauze
while his focus only fits at a point beyond
the curve of the earth.
Or, the reverse condition: think how his stride
could overstep his sight
and how his hands, reaching out idly,
fidgeting perhaps
could destroy an object
that he had never seen.

I am told they look on dwarfs with envy, that
given the chance they would be the smaller thing
but this I am seriously inclined to doubt
for they go on being giants nevertheless.

Some people claim there are no giants. I quote
in fairness the incident that is used as proof:
A giant died – one of the largest – and
his death became a cause of great concern.
To make his coffin the tallest trees were cut,
an acre was set aside as his burial plot.
And after the plot was dug and the trees were felled
somebody thought to measure him and found
the giant in death no taller than himself.

1950s

Photos of a Salt Mine

How innocent their lives look,
how like a child's
dream of caves and winter, both combined:
the steep descent to whiteness
and the stope
with its striated walls
their folds all leaning as if pointing to
the greater whiteness still,
that great white bank
with its decisive front,
that seam upon a slope,
salt's lovely ice.

And wonderful underfoot the snow of salt,
the fine
particles a broom could sweep,
one thinks
muckers might make angels in its drifts,
as children do in snow,
lovers in sheets,
lie down and leave imprinted where they lay
a feathered creature holier than they.

And in the outworked stopes
with lamps and ropes
up miniature Matterhorns
the miners climb,
probe with their lights
the ancient folds of rock –
syncline, anticline –
and scoop from darkness an Aladdin's cave:
rubies and opals glitter from its walls.

But hoses douse the brilliance of these jewels,
melt fire to brine.
Salt's bitter water trickles thin and forms
slow fathoms down
a lake within a cave
lacquered with jet –
white's opposite.
There grey on black the boating miners float
to mend the stays and struts of that old stope
and deeply underground
their words resound,
are multiplied by echo, swell and grow
and make a climate of a miner's voice.

So all the photographs like children's wishes
are filled with caves or winter,
innocence
has acted as a filter,
selected only beauty from the mine.
Except in the last picture, shot
from an acute high angle. In a pit
figures the size of pins are strangely lit
and might be dancing but you know they're not.
Like Dante's vision of the nether hell
men struggle with the bright cold fires of salt
locked in the black inferno of the rock:
the filter here, not innocence but guilt.

1951

The Apple

Look, look, he took me straight
to the snake's eye
to the striped flower
shielding its peppery root.

I said, I shall never go back.

At harvest he took me around and about.
The ground
was apple red and round.
The trees bare.
One apple only hung like a heart in air.

Together bite by bite
we ate,
mouths opposite.
Bit clean through core and all to meet:
through sweet juice met.

I said, I shall never go back.

But someone let an angel down
on a thin string.
It was a rangy paper thing
with one wing torn,
born of a child.

Now, now, we come and go, we come and go,
feverish where that harvest grew.

c. 1951–53

The Event

The keys all turned to that event
as if it were a magnetic lock.
A rush of streams flowed into it
thundering from the great divide
while numberless and hidden heads
like flowers leaned out to feel its light.

The lion, somnolent with food,
the bear in his continuing winter,
rose to its bell as if their blood
conveyed its red and vital current.
That instant the indifferent street
became their sudden food.

Lilies and archangels began
the gradual gentling of the lion.
The burred bear fell asleep again –
a snowfall lulled him to a lamb.
Like velvet toys they lie there prone
and dream the cactus plant of pain.

But children will be born whose blood
remembers that event.
The lion and bear will waken up
ravenous after sleep
and lilies then will be their bread,
archangels their white meat.

1952

Images of Angels

Imagine them as they were first conceived:
part musical instrument and part daisy
in a white manshape.
Imagine a crowd on the Elysian grass
playing ring-around-a-rosy,
mute except for their singing,
their gold smiles
gold sickle moons in the white sky of their faces.
Sex, neither male nor female,
name and race, in each case, simply angel.

Who, because they are white and gold, has made them holy
but never to be loved or petted, never to be friended?

Not children, who imagine them more simply,
see them more coloured and a deal more cosy,
yet somehow mixed with the father, fearful and fully
realized when the vanishing bed
floats in the darkness,
when the shifting point of focus, that drifting star,
has settled in the head.

More easily perhaps, the little notary
who, given one as a pet, could not
walk the sun-dazzled street
with so lamb-white a companion.
For him its loom-large skeleton –
one less articulated than his own –
would dog his days with doom
until behind the lethal lock
used for his legal documents

he guiltily shut it up.
His terror then that it escape
and smiling call for him at work.
Less dreadful for his public shame
worse for his private guilt
if in the hour that he let it out
he found it limp and boneless as a flower.

Perhaps, more certainly perhaps, the financier.
What business man would buy as he buys stock
as many as could cluster on a pin?
Angels are dropping, angels going up.
He could not mouth such phrases and chagrin
would sugar round his lips as he said 'angel'.
For though he mocks their mention he cannot
tie their tinsel image to a tree
without the momentary lowering of his lids
for fear that they exist in worlds which he
uneasy, reconstructs from childhood's memory.

The archaeologist with his tidy science
had he stumbled upon one unawares,
found as he finds an arrowhead, an angel –
a what-of-a-thing
as primitive as a daisy,
might with his ice cold eye have assessed it coolly.
But how, despite his detailed observations
could he face his learned society and explain?
'Gentlemen, it is thought that they are born
with harps and haloes
as the unicorn with its horn.
Study discloses them white and gold as daisies.'

Perhaps only a dog could accept them wholly,
be happy to follow at their heels
and bark and romp with them in the green fields.

Or, take the nudes of Lawrence and impose
asexuality upon them; those
could meet with ease these gilded albinos.

Or a child, not knowing they were angels could
wander along an avenue hand in hand
with his new milk-white playmates,
take a step
and all the telephone wires would become taut
as the high strings of a harp
and space be merely the spaces between strings
and the world mute, except for a thin singing,
as if a sphere – big enough to be in it
and yet small
so that a glance through the lashes
would show it whole –
were fashioned very finely out of wire
and turning in a wind.

But say the angelic word
and *this* innocent
with his almost-unicorn
would let it go –
(even a child would know
that angels should be flying in the sky!)
and feeling implicated in a lie,
his flesh would grow
cold
and snow
would cover the warm and sunny avenue.

1953

T-Bar

Relentless, black on white, the cable runs
through metal arches up the mountain side.
At intervals giant pickaxes are hung
on long hydraulic springs. The skiers ride
propped by the axehead, twin automatons
supported by its handle, one each side.

In twos they move slow motion up the steep
incision in the mountain. Climb. Climb.
Somnambulists, bolt upright in their sleep
their phantom poles swung lazily behind,
while to the right, the empty T-bars keep
in mute descent, slow monstrous jigging time.

Captive the skiers now and innocent,
wards of eternity, each pair alone.
They mount the easy vertical ascent,
pass through successive arches, bride and groom,
as through successive naves, are newly wed
participants in some recurring dream.

So do they move forever. Clocks are broken.
In zones of silence they grow tall and slow,
inanimate dreamers, mild and gentle-spoken
blood-brothers of the haemophilic snow
until the summit breaks and they awaken
imagos from the stricture of the tow.

Jerked from her chrysalis the sleeping bride
suffers too sudden freedom like a pain.
The dreaming bridegroom severed from her side
singles her out, the old wound aches again.
Uncertain, lost, upon a wintry height
these two, not separate, but no longer one.

Now clocks begin to peck and sing. The slow
extended minute like a rubber band
contracts to catapult them through the snow
in tandem trajectory while behind
etching the sky-line, obdurate and slow
the spastic T-bars pivot and descend.

1953

The Masks Are Made by Hand and Show

The masks are made by hand and show
more than the face they're meant to hide.
Friend, mask yourself that I may know
what's going on inside.

c. 1952–53

Social Note

Ordinary people are lovely, they understand
ordinary things, including one another.
They are kindly as anything, they're as kind to you –
whether you want them to be or not – as they are to Mother.

They have real feelings for real things; they grieve at death
and likewise and conversely rejoice at birth.
Ordinary people are real, really they are.
They're the iodized salt of the earth.

Ordinary people are good, they're good as gold
and they don't do anything that isn't good. It doesn't matter
what anyone says to the contrary, ordinary people are good.
In the whole of the wide world only their halves are better.

And they don't discuss politics or religion in case
they might hurt somebody's feelings and anyway
ordinary people can't be bothered and haven't time
and anyway who's interested anyway?

Ordinary people are the most natural people known –
as ordinary as cow parsley or hen bane, *that* natural.
And they want everyone to be just as natural too.
Naturally they're sorry for anyone who isn't natural.

Ordinary people are everywhere and it's so nice
because they can meet other ordinary people without a bother
and from morning to night from beginning to end of their lives
they can all be natural and lovely and kind and good to each other.

1954

Arras

Consider a new habit – classical,
and trees espaliered on the wall like candelabra.
How still upon that lawn our sandalled feet.

But a peacock rattling his rattan tail and screaming
has found a point of entry. Through whose eye
did it insinuate in furled disguise
to shake its jewels and silk upon that grass?

The peaches hang like lanterns. No one joins
those figures on the arras.
                              Who am I
or who am I become that walking here
I am observer, other, Gemini,
starred for a green garden of cinema?

I ask, what did they deal me in this pack?
The cards, all suits, are royal when I look.
My fingers slipping on a monarch's face
twitch and grow slack.
I want a hand to clutch, a heart to crack.

No one is moving now, the stillness is
infinite. If I should make a break …
take to my springy heels … ? But nothing moves.
The spinning world is stuck upon its poles,
the stillness points a bone at me. I fear
the future on this arras.
                              I confess:

It was my eye.
Voluptuous it came.
Its head the ferrule and its lovely tail

folded so sweetly; it was strangely slim
to fit the retina. And then it shook
and was a peacock – living patina,
eye-bright, maculate!
Does no one care?

I thought their hands might hold me if I spoke.
I dreamed the bite of fingers in my flesh,
their poke smashed by an image, but they stand
as if within a treacle, motionless,
folding slow eyes on nothing.
                                While they stare
another line has trolled the encircling air,
another bird assumes its furled disguise.

1954

The Metal and the Flower

Intractable between them grows
a garden of barbed wire and roses.
Burning briars like flames devour
their too innocent attire.
Dare they meet, the blackened wire
tears the intervening air.

Trespassers have wandered through
texture of flesh and petals.
Dogs like arrows moved along
pathways that their noses knew.
While the two who laid it out
find the metal and the flower
fatal underfoot.

Black and white at midnight glows
this garden of barbed wire and roses.
Doused with darkness roses burn
coolly as a rainy moon;
beneath a rainy moon or none
silver the sheath on barb and thorn.

Change the garden, scale and plan:
wall it, make it annual.
There the briary flower grew.
There the brambled wire ran.
While they sleep the garden grows,
deepest wish annuls the will:
perfect still the wire and rose.

1954

This Frieze of Birds

This frieze of birds encloses
Dom. Robert and his
exact embroidery.
Rigidity supplies
a just delineation
of separates, divides
crest, pinions, claws and eyes.
No whole survives such rout.

I have a friend could make
of all this tracery
an intricate poem, neat
as the Lord's Prayer on a pin,
delicate roosters attending
fashioned of glass and tin,
feather of pine, and wattle
most exquisitely brittle.

But for St. Francis, fat,
his brown robe slopping over
like coffee on the grass,
a breakfast of a moment
set in a blur of birds;
for beak and claw and feather
all moltenly together,
my friend would find no words.

And for a field of linnets
greening the thistle or
a snow of cockatoos
upon the mistletoe,
for harlequin rosellas
or magpies domino,
she, grown all string and wire,
a twisted armature

would find them hot and light
as from her metal eye
she saw them in a flight
feathered and fiery
and feel her wire melt
and that small string
frizzle to nothing
as they went pelting by.

1955

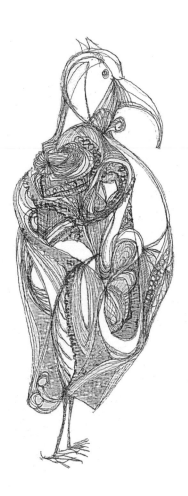

Chimney Fire

Something must be fire for them, these six
brass-helmeted navy-blue navvies come to chop
the old endlessly-polished wainscot with the fireman's axe.
Ready and royal for crisis and climax
shining and stalwart and valiant – for *this*?
Some element in this puny fire must prove
muscled enough for them to pit against,
and so they invade the green room, all six,
square up to its tidy silence and attack.

Only the roar in the brick and that abating
and the place orderly and quiet as a painting
of a house and all their paraphernalia outside waiting
to be used and useless and inside silence growing coolly
as a lily on a green stem.
Oh, how they tackle it, hack it, shout it down
only to find it broken out again,
implacably sending up suckers in the still room,
forevergreen, the chill obverse of flame.

Finally defeat it with their roaring laughter
and helmets on floor and armchair, drinking beer
like an advertisement for a brand name – 'after the fire
the dark blue conqueror relaxes here'
in an abandonment of blue and gold
that Rousseau the Douanier might have set
meticulously upon a canvas – those red brick
faces, vacant, those bright axes
and the weltering dark serge angles of arms and legs.

So they attacked their fire and put it out.
No tendril of silence grew in the green room when they went
into the night like night with only the six
stars of their helmets shining omnipotent
in a fiery constellation
pinking the darkness with a sign unknown
to ride the street like a flume, to fan to flame
smouldering branches of artery and vein
in beautiful conflagration, their lovely dream.

1955

War Lord in the Early Evening

Suitable for a gentleman with medals
to choose for pleasure
and his beneficent care
the long-stemmed roses wilting in the summer weather.

Fitting for a man in his position
to succour them with water
at his side
admiring, dressed in muslin, his small daughter.

He saw the picture clearly. It was charming:
the battered war lord
in the early evening
among the roses, gentle and disarming.

The way he sent the servants for the hoses
they thought a fire was raging
in the garden.
Meanwhile the roses and the light were fading.

Six choppy lengths of tubing were assembled.
Bind them, the general stormed
from six make one.
Was this philosophy? It wasn't plumbing.

How bind six hoses of assorted sizes
all minus fixtures?
Though his servants shrugged
they dropped to a man on their knees and bound their fingers

tightly around the joints and five small fountains
gushed at specific places
on the lawn
and cooled five straining servants' sweating faces.

Pitiful the little thread of water
that trickle, that distil.
The darkness hid
a general toying with a broken water pistol.

Hid from his daughter, frail organza issue
of his now failing loin
the battle done:
so much militia routed in the man.

Sic transit gloria mundi. I would rather
a different finish.
It was devilish
that the devil denied him that one innocent wish.

1955

Giovanni and the Indians

They call to pass the time with Giovanni
and speak an English none can understand
as Giovanni trims the weeping willow,
his ladder teetering in the yellow leaves.

They make him teeter even when he's steady;
their tatters blow and catch him through the trees;
those scraps of colour flutter against stucco
and flash like foreign birds;

and eyes look out at eyes till Giovanni's
are lowered swiftly – one among them is
perhaps the Evil Eye. The weather veers.
Pale leaves flap wetly on the metal trees.

*

Bare winter is pure glass. Past panes of air
he peers but sees no colour flicking raw
behind the little twigs; no movement shakes
the sunlight on the berries, no branch cracks

till quakes of spring unsettle them. Their flocks
emerge, they sprinkle paths with petals.
Now Giovanni pauses, stares and shrugs
hiding behind a golden blind of wattle.

*

One on a cycle, like a ragged sail
that luffs and sags, comes tacking up the hill.
Does Giovanni smile as he darts off, low
over the handlebars of his spinning wheel?

And one, his turban folded like a jug,
and frocked, walks brittle on his blanco'd legs –
a bantam cockerel. Giovanni looks
and laughs and laughs and lurches in great loops

and stoops to bend above a bed and gather
hyacinths, tulips, waterblue and yellow;
passes his offering through the rainy willow
nodding, 'Good fellow,' smiling, 'much good fellow.'

1955

After Rain

The snails have made a garden of green lace:
broderie anglaise from the cabbages,
Chantilly from the choux-fleurs, tiny veils –
I see already that I lift the blind
upon a woman's wardrobe of the mind.

Such female whimsy floats about me like
a kind of tulle, a flimsy mesh,
while feet in gumboots pace the rectangles –
garden abstracted, geometry awash –
an unknown theorem argued in green ink,
dropped in the bath.
Euclid in glorious chlorophyll, half drunk.

I none too sober slipping in the mud
where rigged with guys of rain
the clothes-reel gauche
as the rangy skeleton of some
gaunt delicate spidery mute
is pitched as if
listening;
while hung from one thin rib
a silver web –
its infant, skeletal, diminutive,
now sagged with sequins, pulled ellipsoid,
glistening.

I suffer shame in all these images.
The garden is primeval, Giovanni
in soggy denim squelches by my hub,
over his ruin
shakes a doleful head.

But he so beautiful and diademed,
his long Italian hands so wrung with rain
I find his ache exists beyond my rim
and almost weep to see a broken man
made subject to my whim.

O choir him, birds, and let him come to rest
within this beauty as one rests in love,
till pears upon the bough
encrusted with
small snails as pale as pearls
hang golden in
a heart that knows tears are a part of love.

And choir me too to keep my heart a size
larger than seeing, unseduced by each
bright glimpse of beauty striking like a bell,
so that the whole may toll,
its meaning shine
clear of the myriad images that still –
do what I will – encumber its pure line.

1955

The Glass Air

I dreamed my most extraordinary darling
gangling, come to share
my hot and prairie childhood

the first day loosed the mare from her picket
and rode her bareback
over the little foothills towards the mountains.

And on the second, striding from his tent,
twisted a noose of butcher's string.
Ingenious to my eyes the knots he tied.

The third bright day he laid the slack noose over
the gopher's burrow,
unhurried by the chase,

and lolled a full week, lazy, in the sun
until the head popped, sleek, enquiring.
The noose pulled tight around his throat.

Then the small fur lashed, lit out, hurling
about only to turn
tame silk in his palm

as privy harness, tangled from his pocket
with leash of string
slipped simply on.

But the toy beast and the long rein and the paid-out lengths
of our youth snapped
as the creature jibbed and bit

and the bright blood ran out, the bright blood trickled over,
slowed, grew dark
lay sticky on our skins.

And we two, dots upon that endless plain, Leviathan became
and filled and broke
the glass air like twin figures, vast, in stone.

1956

Bark Drawing

This is a landscape with serifs:

singularly sharp
each emu
kangaroo &
goanna
intaglio
on the bark
of this continent

look in its rivers
fish
swim by in skeleton
fine-boned as a comb

while pin-figured men
string thin
are dancing or hunting

(an alphabet the eye
lifts from the air
as if by ear

two senses
threaded through
a knuckle bone)

stare through
sea water clear
as isinglass or air

there spirit men
giraffid
catch sting ray &
skate
zither-like

or with boomerang
bull roarer &
dillybag

stipple the bark between
zigzag &
herringbone

& in ceremonial
fill the least paddock
with cross-hatch &
serif.

1956

Cook's Mountains

By naming them he made them.
They were there
before he came
but they were not the same.
It was his gaze
that glazed each one.
He saw
the Glass House Mountains in his glass.
They shone.

And they shine still.
We saw them as we drove –
sudden, surrealist, conical
they rose
out of the rain forest.
The driver said,
'Those are the Glass House Mountains up ahead.'

And instantly they altered to become
the sum of shape and name.
Two strangenesses united into one
more strange than either.
Neither of us now
remembers how they looked before they broke
the light to fragments as the driver spoke.

Like mounds of mica,
hive-shaped hothouses,
mountains of mirror glimmering
they form
in diamond panes behind the tree ferns of
the dark imagination,
burn and shake
the lovely light of Queensland like a bell
reflecting Cook upon a deck
his tongue
silvered with paradox and metaphor.

1956

Brazilian House

In this great house white
as a public urinal
I pass my echoing days.
Only the elephant ear leaves
listen outside my window
to the tap of my heels.

Downstairs the laundress
with elephantiasis
sings like an angel
her brown wrists cuffed with suds
and the skinny little black girl
polishing silver laughs to see
her face appear in a tray.

Ricardo, stealthy
lowers his sweating body
into the stream
my car will cross when I
forced by the white porcelain
yammering silence drive
into the hot gold gong
of noonday.

c. 1957–58

Could I Write a Poem Now?

Or am I so
sold to the devil
that a hard frost locks
those lovely waters?

No, scarcely a matter of ice,
but a matter of guilt
having believed
(and pledged my troth)
art is the highest loyalty
and to let
a talent lie about unused
is to break faith.

But how do you write a Chagall?
It boils down to that.

c. 1957–58

Knitters

These women knitting knit a kind of mist –
climate of labyrinth –
into the air.
Sitting like sleepers,
propped against the chintz,
pin-headed somehow – figures by Moore –
arachnes in their webs, they barely stir –

except their eyes and hands, which wired to some
urgent personal circuit,
move as if
a switch controlled them.
Hear the click and hum
as their machines translating hieroglyphs,
compulsive and monotonous, consume –
lozenge and hank – the candy-coloured stuff.

See two observe the ceremony of skeins:
one, forearms raised,
the loops around her palms,
cat's-cradle rocks, is metronome, becalmed;
while her companion
spun from her as from
a wooden spindle, winds a woollen world.

A man rings like an axe, is alien,
imperilled by them,
finds them cold and far.
They count their stitches on a female star
and speak another language,
are not kin.
Or is he Theseus remembering
that maze, those daedal ways, the Minotaur?

They knit him out, the wool grows thick and fills
the room they sit in like a fur
as vegetable more than animal,
surrealist and slightly sinister,
driven by motors strong beyond their wills,
these milky plants devour
more hanks of wool, more cubic feet of air.

c. 1957–58

Some Paintings by Portinari

With the first lot flat
it was as if he'd cut off my breasts
and levelled my nose
like the side of a barn
I walked
        and met them flat
flat on and one
up-tilted my chin.

with the others lord all the colours gone
strange but I wore
red when I came and green
and he made them grey
and painted the grey all over my skin
and the pain
pulled all the muscles and cords.

c. 1957–58

Natural History Museum

I saw a baleen in his bones
long-fingered hands at his sides
I saw him swim in the air like a stone
and I saw through the holes in his face

astraddle a painted tree, in the crook of its wood
the sloths, union-suited in loofah fur
and helmeted too, with only their faces
baby and cretinous, real, as it were.

In a coffin of glass, all the pretty singers
mute on sticks.

The marmosets grow stamens out of their ears
and their fingers feel like the stems of violets
yet a face the size of the top joint of my thumb
like my own from the back of a spoon
looks at me with a wordless question
and in the garden mouth and anus red
our spider guards his golden web.

c. 1957–58

Truce

My enemy in a purple hat
looks suddenly like a plum
and I am dumb with wonder
at the thought
of feuding with a fruit.

c. 1957–58

On Educating the Natives

They who can from palm leaves and from grasses
weave baskets of so intricate a beauty
and simply as a girl combing her hair,
are taught in a square room by a square woman
to cross-stitch on checked gingham.

c. 1957–58

This Whole Green World

This whole green world, crystal and spherical,
silent as the hole in a head, within
which all those birds' coloured beaks cheepcheep
girls' throats yell boys' brakes scream
and Manuel's wheelbarrow crunches and scrapes
its rusty iron rim.

Paint it. The other silence aches around it,
is a green bruise in three dimensions shaped
with compasses and theorems, a slow
chrysoprase fire to gut the head
and leave among the charred curved rafters,
elegant in carbon, a global shell
through which those thousand noises dart like birds.

c. 1957–58

Brazilian Fazenda

That day all the slaves were freed
their manacles, anklets
left on the window ledge to rust in the moist air

and all the coffee ripened
like beads on a bush or balls of fire
as merry as Christmas

and the cows all calved and the calves all lived
such a moo.

On the wide veranda where birds in cages
sang among the bell flowers
I in a bridal hammock
white and tasselled
whistled

and bits fell out of the sky near Nossa Senhora
who had walked all the way in bare feet from Bahía

and the chapel was lit by a child's
fistful of marigolds on the red velvet altar
thrown like a golden ball.

Oh, let me come back on a day
when nothing extraordinary happens
so I can stare
at the sugar-white pillars
and black lace grills
of this pink house.

1966

Cry Ararat!

I

In the dream the mountain near
but without sound.
A dream through binoculars
seen sharp and clear:
the leaves moving, turning
in a far wind
no ear can hear.

First soft in the distance,
blue in blue air
then sharpening, quickening
taking on green.
Swiftly the fingers
seek accurate focus
(the bird
has vanished so often
before the sharp lens
could deliver it)
then as if from the sea
the mountain appears
emerging new-washed
growing maples and firs.
The faraway, here.

Do not reach to touch it
or labour to hear.
Return to your hand
the sense of the hand;
return to your ear
the sense of the ear.
Remember the statue,
that space in the air

which with nothing to hold
what the minute is giving
is through each point
where its marble touches air.

Then will each leaf and flower
each bird and animal
become as perfect as
the thing its name evoked
when busy as a child
the world stopped at the Word
and Flowers more real than flowers
grew vivid and immense;
and Birds more beautiful
and Leaves more intricate
flew, blew and quilted all
the quick landscape.

So flies and blows the dream
embracing like a sea
all that in it swims
when dreaming, you desire
and ask for nothing more
than stillness to receive
the I-am animal,
the We-are leaf and flower,
the distant mountain near.

II

So flies and blows the dream that haunts us when we wake
to the unreality of bright day:
the far thing almost sensed by the still skin
and then the focus lost, the mountain gone.
This is the loss that haunts our daylight hours
leaving us parched at nightfall

blowing like last year's leaves
sibilant on blossoming trees
and thirsty for the dream of the mountain
more real than any event:
more real than strangers passing on the street
in a city's architecture white as bone
or the immediate companion.

But sometimes there is one
raw with the dream of flying:
'I, a bird,
landed that very instant
and complete –
as if I had drawn a circle in my flight
and filled its shape –
find air a perfect fit.
But this my grief,
that with the next tentative lift
of my indescribable wings
the ceiling looms
heavy as a tomb.

'Must my most exquisite and private dream
remain unleavened?
Must this flipped and spinning coin that sun
could gild and make miraculous become
so swiftly pitiful?
The vision of the flight it imitates
burns brightly in my head as if a star
rushed down to touch me where I stub against
what must forever be my underground.'

III

These are the dreams that haunt us,
these the fears.
Will the grey weather wake us,
toss us twice in the terrible night to tell us
the flight is cancelled
and the mountain lost?

O, then cry Ararat!

The dove believed
in her sweet wings and in the rising peak
with such a washed and easy innocence
that she found rest on land for the sole of her foot
and, silver, circled back,
a green twig in her beak.

The leaves that make the tree by day,
the green twig the dove saw fit
to lift across a world of water
break in a wave about our feet.
The bird in the thicket with his whistle
the crystal lizard in the grass
the star and shell
tassel and bell
of wild flowers blowing where we pass,
this flora-fauna flotsam, pick and touch,
requires the focus of the total I.

A single leaf can block a mountainside;
all Ararat be conjured by a leaf.

1966

Dark Kingdom

Deep swings the midnight arc.
These heavens spin below
in giddying zodiac.

What constellations burn?
The Chalice and the Goat,
the Sceptered Unicorn.

Pinned to a turning sphere
I know not up nor down.
I dizzy as I stare.

Wheeling around a point
that drives me through and through
the very stars grow faint.

Such blacknesses abound
I know not in nor out.
O Shadow, take my hand.

Emblazon on the night
resplendent – though I drown –
the Crowned Hermaphrodite.

1966

The

Ancient nomadic snowman has rolled round.
His spoor: a wide swathe on the white ground
signs of a wintry struggle where he stands.

Stands? Yes, he stands. What snowman sat?
Legless, indeed, but more as if he had
legs than had not.

White double O, white nothing nothing, this
the child's first man on a white paper, his
earliest and fistful image is

now three-dimensional. Abstract. Everyman.
Of almost manna, he is still no man
no person, this so personal snowman.

O transient un-inhabitant, I know
no child who, on seeing the leprous thaw
undo your whitened torso and face of snow

would not, had he the magic
call you back
from that invisible attack

even knowing he can, with the new miracle
of another and softer and whiter snowfall
make you again, this time more wonderful.

Snowman

Innocent single snowman. Overnight
brings him – a bright
omen – a thunderbolt of white.

But once I saw a mute in every yard
come like a plague; a stock-still multitude
and all stone-buttoned, bun-faced and absurd.

And next day they were still there but each
had changed a little as if all had inched
forward or back, I barely knew which;

and greyed a little too, grown sinister
and disreputable in their sooty fur,
numb, unmoving and nothing moving near.

And as far as I could see the snow was scarred
only with angels' wing marks or the feet of birds
like twigs broken upon the snow or shards

discarded. And I could hear no sound
as far as I could hear except a round
kind of echo without end

rung like a hoop below them and above
jarring the air they had no need of
in a landscape without love.

from 1958 to 1967

A Backwards Journey

When I was a child of say, seven,
I still had serious attention to give
to everyday objects. The Dutch Cleanser –
which was the kind my mother bought –
in those days came in a round container
of yellow cardboard around which ran
the very busy Dutch Cleanser woman
her face hidden behind her bonnet
holding a yellow Dutch Cleanser can
on which a smaller Dutch Cleanser woman
was holding a smaller Dutch Cleanser can
on which a minute Dutch Cleanser woman
held an imagined Dutch Cleanser can …

This was no game. The woman led me
backwards through the eye of the mind
until she was the smallest point
my thought could hold to. And at that moment
I think I knew that if no one called
and nothing broke the delicate jet
of my attention, that tiny image
could smash the atom of space and time.

1969

Another Space

Those people in a circle on the sand
are dark against its gold
turn like a wheel
revolving in a horizontal plane
whose axis – do I dream it? –
vertical
invisible
immeasurably tall
rotates a starry spool.

Yet *if* I dream
why in the name of heaven are fixed parts
within me set in motion
like a poem?

Those people in a circle reel me in.
Down the whole length of golden beach I come
willingly pulled by their rotation
slow
as a moon pulls waters
on a string
their turning circle winds around its rim.

I see them there in three dimensions yet
their height implies another space
their clothes'
surprising chiaroscuro postulates
a different spectrum.
What kaleidoscope
does air construct
that all their movements make a compass rose
surging and altering?
I speculate
on some dimension I can barely guess.

Nearer I see them dark-skinned.
They are dark. And beautiful.
Great human sunflowers spinning in a ring
cosmic as any bumble-top
the vast
procession of the planets in their dance.
And nearer still I see them – 'a Chagall' –
each fiddling on an instrument – its strings
of some black woollen fibre
and its bow – feathered –
an arrow almost.
                    Arrow *is*.

For now the headman – one step forward – shoots
(or does he bow or does he lift a kite
up and over the bright pale dunes of air?)
to strike the absolute centre of my skull
my absolute centre somehow
with such skill
such staggering lightness
that the blow is love.

And something in me melts.
It is as if a glass partition melts –
or something I had always thought was glass –
some pane that halved my heart
is proved, in its melting, ice.

And to-fro all the atoms pass
in bright osmosis
hitherto
in stasis locked
where now a new
direction opens like an eye.

1969

Fly: On Webs

Two kinds of web: the one
not there. A sheet of glass.
Look! I am flying through air,
spinning in emptiness ... SPUNG!
... bounced on a flexible wire,
caught by invisible guys.

The other a filigree, gold
as the call of a trumpet. A sun
to my myriad-faceted eye.
A season. A climate. Compelled
and singing hosannas I fly:
I dazzle. I struggle. I drown.

1969

Knitter's Prayer

Unknit me –
all those blistering strange small intricate stitches –
shell stitch, moss stitch, pearl and all too plain;
unknit me to the very first row of ribbing,
let only the original simple knot remain.

Then let us start again.

1969

Travellers' Palm

Miraculously plaited tree.
A sailor's knot
rooted,
a growing fan
whose grooved and slanted branches
are aqueducts
end-stopped
for tropical rains.

Knot, fan,
Quixote's windmill,
what-you-will –
for me, traveller,
a well.

On a hot day I took
a sharp and pointed knife,
plunged,
and water gushed
to my cupped mouth

old water
tasting green,
of vegetation and dust,
old water, warm as tears.

And in that tasting,
taster, water, air,
in temperature identical
were so
intricately merged
a fabulous foreign bird
flew silent from a void

lodged in my boughs.

1969

Leather Jacket

One day the King laid hold on one of the peacocks
and gave orders that he should be sewn up in a leather jacket.
SUHRAWARDI

That peacock a prisoner
that many-eyed bird
blind.

Enclosed in a huge leather purse.
Locked in darkness.
All its pupils sealed
its tiny brain sealed
its light and fluttering heart
heavy as a plum.

Its life vegetable.
That beautiful colourful bird
a root vegetable.

Cry, cry for the peacock
hidden in heavy leather
sewn up in heavy leather
in the garden

among flowers
and flowering trees
near streams
and flowering fountains
among cicadas
and singing birds.

The peacock sees nothing
smells nothing
hears nothing at all
remembers nothing
but a terrible yearning
a hurt beyond bearing
an almost memory
of a fan of feathers
a growing garden

and sunshine falling
as light as pollen.

1970

Anachronism

The wind plucked a dying leaf from a palm tree.
It fell like the feather of a giant bird,
superimposed pre-history upon the third
month of the year nineteen sixty-three
and made an anachronism of me.

1970

Three Gold Fish

I feel quite sure those three gold fish I saw
burning like Blake's *Tyger* in the pool
were real all right.
The pool was different too.
It seemed to swell
like some great crystalline and prismed tear
and brim and never spill
and those fish burned within it
burned and shone
and left their brand –
a piscine fleur-de-lys –
stamped on the air, on me,
on skin and hair
spinning to giddy heaven.

Sharp and clear
that fiery image burns within me still:
those three gold fish
the pool
the altered air
and I – observing and observed –
a high
point on a twirling spindle which
spun and hurled great gilded lariats.

1970

Ecology

If a boy
eats an apple
because a bee
collects nectar,
what happens
because a boy
eats an apple?

1970

Beside You

1.
I lay beside you
soft and white as dough
put by to rise

I rose and rose and rose

2.
We sounded *e*
above high *c*
the note
broke all my crystal
in a flash
smashed your plate glass

3.
My body flowers
in blossoms
that will fall
petal by petal
all the days of my life

1970s

Let the Honey Accumulate

Let the honey accumulate in the comb
Let it not leak or drizzle away
Let the bear's paw not encounter it
Let the bear's snout not enter it

Let the gold accumulate in the treasury
Let the Queen embroider with golden thread
Let the King's robe stand stiff with it
Let the child's hair shine bright with it

Let the dough rise in the kitchen
Let it double its bulk
Let it rise again in the hot oven
And become a loaf with a golden crust

1970s

Picking Daffodils

They have spilled their slippery juices over me
let fall saliva from their long green stems
Their viscous threads of water swing into my house

remind me of the waters of your mouth

1970s

122

Neighbours

stunned
by bright leaves
as sun
broke out a moment
from a swollen sky
and fired dull ochre
into gold

I
mid-phrase (or
you were)
on the phone
forgot
what we were saying
overbrimmed
into our shining gardens –
grey birds silver in
the beaten leaves
webs of spiders
gleaming
and the last
crabbed apples
embers
in the trees'
transfigured ash

1970s

Preparation

Go out of your mind.
Prepare to go mad.
Prepare to break
split along cracks
inhabit the darks of your eyes
inhabit the whites.

Prepare to be huge.
Be prepared to be small
the least molecule of
an unlimited form.
Be a limited form
and spin in your skin
one point in its whole.

Be prepared to prepare
for what you have dreamed
to burn and be burned
to burst like a pod
to break at your seams.

Be pre-pared. And pre-pare.
But it's never like that.
It is where you are not
that the fissure occurs
and the light crashes in.

1971

The Yellow People in Metamorphosis

Lunar Phase

Not only silvered
One dimension less

Moon's light
falls thin and flat

on metal shapes
that heave and strive

immobile
but alive

Earthly Phase

i

In topazes and amber
mango, peach
the yellow people hive
the yellow people swarm
just beyond our hearing
just beyond our sight
Their chromosomes
and yellow genes
squeezed from a tube
of cadmium
their canary-coloured
hair and skin
and eyes
are palest
cadmium

Molecular
they stretch and grow
Don waggish wigs
wear caps, capes, cloaks
gamboge and chrome
Crave mosaics
small moorish patterns
checks   greek key
all intricate shapes
fine mottle   stipple
singing reeds
whistles of birds

Whose notes are these?
That trill? Did (s)he
flicker a yellow throat muscle?
Do wiry yellow curls vibrate?
A springed instrument? Is s(he)
crossed with a flute?
That crown
a splendid yellow bony comb
grown from the cranium

The yellow people hive
the yellow people swarm
just beyond our hearing
just beyond belief

Warblers in the leaves?
Peaches in the trees?
An antic
trick
of light?

ii

Stamp   Stamp   I feel them weighty
Wonderful acrobats clanking about
loud in the next dimension
luring my inner eye
and growing huge and yellow
Ballooning gunny-sacks
striving to sunhood
not yet sunny
rayed
as dandelions
and lighter far
than their looming size suggests
See them throw ballast up to another ether
Ascend
hand over fist

Yet one least glance aside
shows me their scale of gold
ladders that come and go
They alter as they climb
and shining chains and cones
reach down to draw them up
as   known to unknown spanned
with weightless veins and bones
transforming all their yellow
they golden   glow
and
        vanish

iii

An orison of them stars my farthest heaven

Vertical
these almost alchemists
gilders of nimbi
leaf the chieftain's feathers
sol's flames   cock's crest
bright leo's sunburst locks

Make sovereign all my pocketful of copper

Solar Phase

This is another matter
Seventh heaven
Among celestial celandines to eat
one apple for eternity

(I know
nothing of what I speak
I speak
nothing of what I know)

1972

Stefan

Stefan
aged eleven
looked at the baby and said
When he thinks it must be pure thought
because he hasn't any words yet
and we
proud parents
admiring friends
who had looked at the baby

looked at the baby again

1973

Masqueraders

What curious masks we wear:
bald patches and grey hair
who once wore dark or fair.

Wear too much flesh or none –
a scrag of skin and bone.
The gold gone.

Bifocalled and watch-bound
who once, time out of mind
glimpsed world without end.

Worse masquerades to come:
white cane, black gaping tomb
as if we were blind, dead, lame

who, in reality, are
dark, fair and shinier
than the masks we wear or wore.

1973

Spinning

Hurl your giant thunderbolt that on my heart
falls gently as a feather, falls and fills
each crease and cranny of me – a chinook:
sweet water, head to foot.

With lightning stagger me so I may stand
centred as never otherwise. In stock-
stillness, dizzying movement find.
Spinning, a dot.

All-of-a-piece, seamless; with the warp and woof
afterwards/before. The stuff spun
without stop or selvedge – measureless
continuum.

Visible/invisible. Golden. Clear
as any crystal. How to name it? How
to loose or hold – for held is holder here
and holder held.

Harry me. Hurry me to spaces where
my Father's house has many dimensions.
Tissue of tesseract.
A sphered sphere.

1973

Shaman

Now to be healed of an old wound requires
diet, cautery, exercise and spells.

The shaman is solemn.
He burns herbs.
The air is moiréed, rainbowed even.
I am chilled.
In the folds of his intricate robes
of feathers, furs
beads like a bird's eyes
pale polished bone,
his curled hands lie
one upon the other, relaxed, as if asleep.
Hands curiously painted with my name and yours.

Messages are transmitted mind to mind.
For just as long as he wishes
my mind twins his.
Small images of you form and fill my head
they are leaden images and heavy as lead
weigh down my eyelids
weigh down my head
torso, arms, legs, feet.
I am a dead weight held fast to the dead.
White wires pin and bind me.
Am I asleep?

He prescribes salves and potions, uses words
from another language.
The lines of his face spell out undecipherable messages.
When he opens his lips to speak he displays a jade
green satiny lining to his mouth and throat.
Is he *Diphyllodes magnificus* in disguise?
Tropical? Pied plumage of paradise?
I am no longer certain.
Is he man? Or bird?

It is all that twittering perhaps.
Short vowels. Long.
Quick clicking consonants.
Inscrutable eyes
bright as black currants.
Tall curious plumes
nodding as he moves.
Faint peppery whiff of dung.

1973

Finches Feeding

They fall like feathered cones from the tree above,
sumi the painted grass where the birdseed is,
skirl like a boiling pot
or a shallow within a river –
a bar of gravel breaking the water up.

Having said that, what have I said?
Not much.

Neither my delight nor the length of my watching is conveyed
and nothing profound recorded, yet these birds
as I observe them
stir such feelings up –
such yearnings for weightlessness, for hollow bones,
rapider heartbeat, east/west eyes
and such wonder – seemingly half remembered – as they rise
spontaneously into air, like feathered cones.

1974

Macumba: Brazil

they are cleaning the chandeliers
they are waxing the marble floors
they are rubbing the golden faucets
they are burnishing brazen doors
they are polishing forks in the *copa*
they are praising the silver trays

their jerkins are striped like hornets
their eyes are like black wax

they are changing the salt in the cupboards
they are cooking *feijão* in the kitchen
they are cutting tropical flowers
they are buying herbs at the market
they are stealing a white rooster
they are bargaining for a goat

they are dressed in white for macumba
their eyes are like black coals

they are making a doll of wax
they are sticking her full of pins
they are dancing to the drums
they are bathed in the blood of the rooster
they are lighting the beach with candles
they are wading into the ocean
with presents for Iemanjá

they are dressed in the salt of the ocean
their eyes are like bright flames

they are giving her gifts of flowers
they are throwing her tubes of lipstick
they are offering shoes and scarves
brassieres and sanitary napkins
whatever a woman needs
they are flinging themselves on the waters
and singing to Iemanjá

they are drenched and white for macumba
and their eyes are doused and out

1976

Phone Call from Mexico

Over the years and miles   your
voice   weeping
telling me you are old
have lost your mind
and all the winds and waters of
America
sound in your words

I see your house
a square-cut topaz   set
within a larger   square
tangle of garden
walled
Brick walks
wild dahlias
raspberry canes and dogs
Raised ladies' flowerbeds
crammed with mignonettes
lobelias
little red-eyes
all the buzz
and hum of summer
It is hot
The golden sun rains down
its golden dust ·
upon you   shrunken
toothless   lonely   I
do not know this
person
Elinor
Don't know   can't see
you as you say you are
a shrivelled pod
rattling   rasping
a crazed creature
dazed

butting the golden air
with your goat's head
crying against
your gods your gods your gods
whom once you sensed
benign caretakers of
the realms   dominions of
your provenance
and now know baneful
black   obsidian
to be confronted
and destroyed

How tell you they
are ungods
Elinor?
How urge you to unlock
and put aside
your clumsy armour
manic armaments
and impotent blind rage?
to lay your head
down gently
like a quarrelsome
tired child?

A phone call
will not do
cannot give comfort   can
not thorns extract
nor antidote
force down
Over this distance
cannot touch your hand

Your voice is broken arrows
You are all
those whom I love
who age ungainly
whose
joints   hearts   psyches
minds   unhinge
and whom
I cannot mend
or ease

How do we end
this phone call
Elinor?
You
railing and roiling
over miles and years
And I
in tears

1976

Seraphim

In the dream it was the seraphim who came
golden, six-winged
with eyes of aquamarine
and set my hair aflame
and spoke in a language which written down –
an elegant script of candelabras and chalices –
spelled out my name

but it was not my name

The mornings following were bright as wings
sky's intricate cirrus
the feathers under his wings
the wind's great rush
the bladed beat of his wings

Mare's tails traced the passage of his seraphic chariot

Hummingbirds ruby-throated roared and braked
in the timeless isinglass air and burned like coals
high in the fronds of a brass palm sunbirds sang
girasoles swung their cadmium-coloured hair
and I heard the seraphim telling once again
the letters of my name

but my name was lost in the spoken syllables

1976

Dwelling Place

This habitation – bones and flesh and skin –
where I reside, proceeds through sun and rain
a mobile home with windows and a door
and pistons plunging, like a soft machine.

Conforming as a bus, its 'metal' is
more sensitive than chrome or brass. It knows
a pebble in its shoe or heat or cold.
I scrutinize it through some aperture

that gives me godsview – see it twist and change.
It sleeps, it weeps, its poor heart breaks,
it dances like a bear, it laughs, opines
(and therefore *is*). It has a leafy smell

of being young in all the halls of heaven.
It serves a term in anterooms of hell,
greying and losing lustre. It is dull.
A lifeless empty skin. I plot its course

and watch it as it moves – a house, a bus;
I, its inhabitant, indweller – eye
to that tiny chink where two worlds meet –
or – if you so discern it – two divide.

1976

The Flower Bed

Circular –
at a guess, twelve feet across –
and filled with a forest of sunflowers.
Girasoles turned sunward, yellow-lashed
black eyes staring at the sailing Sun.
No prospect of a blink
no fall or shift,
the focus constant, eye to eye engaged
as human eye can lock with human eye
and find within its ever-widening core,
such vastnesses of space
one's whole self tumbles in.

I see it in a glass or through a port,
crystalline,
refracting, like a globe,
its edges bending, sides distorted,
shine
of a thick lens,
the peep-hole through a door in which I *saw*
a tiny man
but *see* a bed of flowers
as bright as if enamelled yellow & green,
shooting their eye-beams at their Lord the Sun,
like so much spider's silk stretched true and taut.

And my own yellow eye, black lashed, provides
triangulation. We enmesh
three worlds with our geometry.
I learn,
in timeless Time at their green leafy school,
such silks & stares
such near-invisible straight curving lines
curving like Space itself
which merge and cross at the Omega point
and double back
to make transparent, multifoliate
Flowers of the Upper Air.

1976

A Grave Illness

Someone was shovelling gravel all that week.
The flowering plums came out.
Rose-coloured streets
branched in my head –
spokes of a static wheel
spinning and whirring only when I coughed.
And sometimes, afterwards, I couldn't tell
if I had coughed or he had shovelled. Which.

Someone was shovelling until it hurt.
The rasp of metal on cement, the scrape
and fall
of all that broken rock.
Such industry day after day. For what?
My cough's accompanist?
The flowering trees
blossomed behind my eyes in drifts of red
delicate petals. I was hot.
The shovel grated in my breaking chest.

Someone was shovelling gravel. Was it I?
Burying me in shifts and shards of rock
up to my gasping throat. My head was out
dismembered, sunken-eyed
as John the Baptist's on a plate.
Meanwhile the plum
blossoms trickling from above
through unresistant air
fell on my eyes and hair
as crimson as my blood.

1976

The Selves

Every other day I am an invalid.
Lie back among the pillows and white sheets
lackadaisical O lackadaisical.
Brush my hair out like a silver fan.
Allow myself to be wheeled into the sun.
Calves'-foot jelly, a mid-morning glass of port,
these I accept and rare azaleas in pots.

The nurses humour me. They call me 'dear'.
I am pilled and pillowed into another sphere
and there my illness rules us like a queen,
is absolute monarch, wears a giddy crown
and I, its humble servant at all times, am its least
serf on occasion and excluded from the feast.

Every other *other* day I am as fit
as planets circling.
I brush my hair into a golden sun,
strike roses from a bush,
rare plants in pots
blossom within the green of my eyes, I am
enviable O I am enviable.

Somewhere in between the two, a third
wishes to speak, cannot make itself heard,
stands unmoving, mute, invisible,
a bolt of lightning in its naked hand.

1976

Motel Pool

The plump good-natured children play in the blue pool:
roll and plop; plop and roll;

slide and tumble, oiled, in the slippery sun
silent as otters, turning over and in,

churning the water; or – seamstresses – cut and sew
with jackknives its satins invisibly.

Not beautiful, but suddenly limned with light
their elliptical wet flesh in a flash reflects it

and it greens the green grass, greens the hanging leaf
greens Adam and Eden, greens little Eve.

1977

The Disguises

You, my Lord, were dressed in astonishing disguises:
as a Chinese emperor, ten feet tall,
as a milk-skinned woman
parading in exquisite stuffs.

You were ambiguous and secret
and hidden in other faces.

How did we know you were there at all?
Your ineffable presence
perfumed the air like an avenue of lilacs.

1977

Domestic Poem for a Summer Afternoon

The yellow garden-chair is newly webbed.
There, Arthur, full-length, reads of 'Toronto the Golden',
dozes, nods, lets fall his magazine.
From a golden book I read of Arthur, the King,
and Taliessen, the King's poet. I dream of the crown.
Was it jewelled with rubies, emeralds, stones the colour of his eyes?

The ducks are within arm's reach as usual
at this time in the afternoon – two mallards, webbed
feet tucked out of sight, they float
in unreflecting emerald grass. They doze.
Might be decoys, these wild water birds
unmoving as wood.

It is hot. Siesta still.
Not hot enough for Brazil but I think of Brazil
and the small yellow bird that flew in and perched
on the toe of Arthur's crossed-over foot,
puffed out its feathers, settled down for the night;
and the hummingbird, ruby-throated, a glowing coal
with the noise of a jet
that landed cool and light on the crown of his head.

We are settled down for the afternoon,
with whispering sprinklers and whirring jets.
We are so motionless we might be decoys
placed here by higher hunters who watch from their blind.
Arthur asleep has the face of a boy.
Like blue obsidian the drake's head glints.
His mate and I are brown in feather and skin
and above us the midsummer sun, crown of the sky,
shines indiscriminate down on duck and man.

1977

About Death

1.

And at the moment of death
what is correct procedure?

Cut the umbilical, they said.

And with the umbilical cut
how then prepare the body?

Wash it in sacred water.
Dress it in silk for the wedding.

2.

I wash and iron for you
your final clothes
(my heart on your sleeve)
wishing to wash your flesh
wishing to close
your sightless eyes

nothing remains to do

I am a vacant house.

1978

After Reading *Albino Pheasants* by Patrick Lane

Pale beak … pale eye … the dark imagination
flares like magnesium. Add but *pale flesh*
and I am lifted to a weightless world:
watered cerulean, chrome-yellow (light)
and green, veronese – if I remember – a soft wash
recalls a summer evening sky.

At Barra de Navidad we watched the sky
fade softly like a bruise. Was it imagination
that showed us Venus phosphorescent in a wash
of air and ozone? – a phosphorescence flesh
wears like a mantle in bright moonlight,
a natural skin-tone in that other world.

Why should I wish to escape this world?
Why should three phrases alter the colour of the sky
the clarity, texture even, of the light?
What is there about the irrepressible imagination
that the adjective *pale* modifying *beak, eye* and *flesh*
can set my sensibilities awash?

If with my thickest brush I were to lay a wash
of thinnest watercolour I could make a world
as unlike my own dense flesh
as the high-noon midsummer sky;
but it would not catch at my imagination
or change the waves or particles of light

yet *pale* can tip the scales, make light
this heavy planet. If I were to wash
everything I own in mercury, would imagination
run rampant in that suddenly silver world –
free me from gravity, set me floating sky-
ward – thistledown – permanently disburdened of my flesh?

Like cygnets hatched by ducks, our minds and flesh
are imprinted early – what to me is light
may be dark to one born under a sunny sky.
And however cool the water my truth won't wash
without shrinking except in its own world
which is one part matter, nine parts imagination.

I fear flesh which blocks imagination,
the light of reason which constricts the world.
Pale beak … pale eye … pale flesh … My sky's awash.

1978

Message

This message trims the world
drives home its loosening bolts
tightens its slackening screws:

none but the Messenger
can send a kiss by messenger.

1978

Evening Dance of the Grey Flies

Grey flies, fragile, slender-winged and slender-legged
scribble a pencilled script across the sunlit lawn.

As grass and leaves grow black
the grey flies gleam –
their cursive flight a gold calligraphy.

It is the light that gilds their frail
bodies, makes them fat and bright as bees –
reflected or refracted light –

as once my fist
burnished by some beam I could not see
glowed like gold mail and conjured Charlemagne

as once your face
grey with illness and with age –
a silverpoint against the pillow's white –

shone suddenly like the sun
before you died.

1978

The First Part (excerpt)

Great desire to write it all.
Is it age, death's heavy breath
making absolute autobiography
urgent?

Who would think that this old hive
housed such honey?
Could one guess
blue and gold of a macaw
blue and gold of sky and sun
could set up such melodic din
beat so musical a drum?

Distilled from all this living,
all this gold.

  .   .   .   .

5. Lost ring. Lost ring.
   She lost it. Lost it.
   Pain
   of that loss
   lay on us
   summerlong.
   And then to my bright eye
   the gleam in the grass.
   The gold in the green
   beneath the snow-apple tree.

I glimpsed the changed
geometry of Eden.
Transparent bird
in its transparent shell.

  .   .   .   .

8. Agates and alleys. Smokies. Glassies.
    Tumbling galaxies of them. Worlds.
    A dark disappearing one that whirled
    and a spiral one that drew me in
    to vanishing point at its poles.

9. Backdrop: the cordillera of the Rockies.
    Infinity – slowly spinning in the air –
    invisibly entered through the holes of gophers,
    visibly, in a wigwam's amethyst smoke.

    Eternity implicit on the prairie.
    One's self the centre of a boundless dome
    so balanced in its horizontal plane
    and sensitively tuned that one's least move
    could fractionally tip it North, South, East.

    Westward, in undulations of beige turf,
    the fugal foothills changed their rhythm, rose
    to break in fire and snow. My Hindu Kush.

    It was a landscape in which things could grow
    enormous. Full of struts. A prairie sky
    builds an immense Meccano
    piling high
    shapes its horizon levels.

.   .   .   .

12. Wind whipping us, rain pricking,
    poplars bending.
    Through a stream of all my hair,
    gleam of my father's spurs,
    our jingling bridles,
    the grave-box, lidless, open
    where we rode:

    string figure in bangles and rags.
    Small corpse picked to the bone.

    Dusk fell.
    In all my cells dusk fell.

    My shroud or winding sheet.

    O bind me
    tight against this eye
    this prairie eye
    that stares and stares.

    O hide me safe
    in cleft or coulee

    fold me
    in leaves or blowing
    grasses.

    Hold me.

    Hold me.

1979

George Johnston Reading

A slow January, grey, the weather rainy.
Day after day after day the ceiling zero.
Then you arrive, comb honey from your hives pulled from
your suitcase, head full of metrics, syllable count,
rhyme – half-hidden, half rhyme and alliteration –
the poem's skeleton and ornamentation –
to give a reading as untheatrical as
it is subtle, elegant and unexpected.

I had not anticipated your translations
from Old Norse, your saga of heroic Gisli –
good man, strong man, man who could split an enemy
as butchers split a chicken, clean through the breastbone –
driven to running bloody, head drenched in redness,
dreamer of dark dreams prophetic of his downfall.
Writer of skaldic verses. Gisli, crow-feeder.
Great Gisli, dead of great wounds, son of whey-Thorbjorn.

Nor had I been prepared for those skaldic verse forms
(three-stressed lines in four pairs, final foot trochaic)
that made my head hum – their intricate small magic
working away like yeast till eight lines of court metre
are glittering and airy, furnished with pianos,
each short line, inexplicably a pianist
recreating for me the music of Scarlatti –
crossing hands on the keyboard, crossing and crossing.

Or – working away like bees in blossoms, shaking
a pollen of consonants on the audience
which sat, bundled and bunched in mufflers and greatcoats
in the bare unwelcoming hall where poets read
in Victoria, city of rainy winters.
And thinking about it now, I remember sun
and how honey sweetened the verses, made them gold
and tasting, that mid-January, of field-flowers.

1979

Entreaty

O, Image-Maker
                    throw
your bridal flowers.

1980

Out Here: Flowering

I have not been a tree long enough yet.

JONATHAN GRIFFIN

Such stern weather. Metallic. When I was a human child
my surrogate mother smiled like that –
frostily from stone eyes – no heart in it –
a withering blasted cold
that coated me with ice – I, a small tree glistening in a field
of glassy snow – shot
beautifully through with rainbows and somehow – absolute.
But spoiled. Utterly spoiled.

No wonder the blossoming has been slow,
the springs like flares, the crowding flowers
a surfeit of whipped cream. How many years have I stood sere
brown and unseasonable in the subliming air?
But now the melt has begun and the weather pours
over me in a pelt of petalled snow.

1980

Star-Gazer

The very stars are justified.
The galaxy
italicized.

I have proofread
and proofread
the beautiful script.

There are no
errors.

1980

The Filled Pen

Eager to draw again,
find space in that small room
for my drawing-board and inks
and the huge revolving world
the delicate nib releases.

I have only to fill my pen
and the shifting gears begin:
flywheel and cogwheel start
their small-toothed interlock

and whatever machinery draws
is drawing through my fingers
and the shapes that I have drawn
gaze up into my eyes.
We stare each other down.

Light of late afternoon –
white wine across my paper –
the subject I would draw.
Light of the stars and sun.

Light of the swan-white moon.
The blazing light of trees.
And the rarely glimpsed bright face
behind the apparency of things.

1980

Custodian

I watch it.
Lock and stock.
No joke.
It is my job.

I dust, I wash, I guard
this fading fibre;
polish even.
Spit.

And rub I it
and shine
and wear it to the bone.
Lay bare its nub.

It is but matter
and it matters not
one whit or tittle
if I wear it out.

Yet mend I it and darn
and patch
and pat it even
like a dog

that which the Auctioneer
when I am gone,
for nearly nought
will knock down
from his block.

1981

Ours

For Patrick Anderson – d. 1979

At something over sixty he is dead
and I, a friend of his twenties,
I am still – tentatively – here.

'Friend'. Were we friends?
Our alliance something less:
acquaintances who knew each other well
and met each other often,
warmed by the same blaze.

Sparked by his singular talent
my small fires
angered him.

He wished me near,
appreciative of his skills,
aficionada of good writing.
His good writing.
Not to write well.

Hard to be friends.
Ditches and hedges between.

And yet, at times
our hearts both leapt
in love with metaphor,
or we laughed, played verbal handball,
eyes locked. We were friends.

Now he is dead.
And I think of the breath
he breathed into his poems
and of how
with nothing passing for love between us
something passed
something memorable and alive –
a kind of walking bird
which, when we least expected,
would suddenly take flight.

His and mine, that bird. Ours.
Now
unable to fly.

1981

This Sky

Tonight
beneath this sky
I could plunge my hands
in snow
and pull forth goldfish.

1981

Concentration

Shall I break the bones of my head
in a nutcracker?
Brain-break. Mind-break.

The room in a trice turns black.

The fontanelles open
a fraction of a second

something shimmering whizzes out.

1984

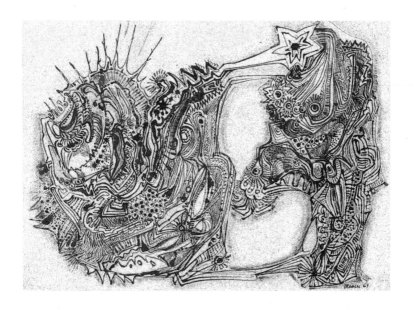

Deaf Mute in the Pear Tree

His clumsy body is a golden fruit
pendulous in the pear tree

Blunt fingers among the multitudinous buds

Adriatic blue the sky above and through
the forking twigs

Sun ruddying tree's trunk, his trunk
his massive head thick-nobbed with burnished curls
tight-clenched in bud

(Painting by Generalić. Primitive.)

I watch him prune with silent secateurs

Boots in the crotch of branches shift their weight
heavily as oxen in a stall

Hear small inarticulate mews from his locked mouth
a kitten in a box

Pear clippings fall
                    soundlessly on the ground
Spring finches sing
                    soundlessly in the leaves

A stone. A stone in ears and on his tongue

Through palm and fingertip he knows the tree's
quick springtime pulse

Smells in its sap the sweet incipient pears

Pale sunlight's choppy water glistens on
his mutely snipping blades

and flags and scraps of blue
above him make regatta of the day

But when he sees his wife's foreshortened shape
sudden and silent in the grass below
uptilt its face to him

then air is kisses, kisses

stone dissolves

his locked throat finds a little door

and through it feathered joy
flies screaming like a jay

1984

Invisible Presences Fill the Air

I hear the clap of their folding wings
like doors banging or wooden shutters.
They land and settle – giant birds
on the epaulettes of snowed-on statues.

On grass one drops its greenest feather.
On the head of a blond boy, a yellow.
The red feather on my heart falls plumb.
Do not ask about the whitest feather.

I feel them breathing on my cheek.
They are great horses dreaming of flight.
They crowd against me. Are outsize.
Smell of sweet grass. Smell of hay.

When in my heart their hooves strike flint
a fire rages through my blood.
I want water. I want wool.
I want the fruits of citrus trees.

Their eyes flash me such mysteries
that I am famished, am ill-clad.
Dressed in the rags of my party clothes
I gather their hairs for a little suit.

O who can name me their secret names?
Anael, opener of gates.
Phorlakh, Nisroc, Heiglot,
Zlar.

1984

Visitants

Each afternoon at four bird after bird
soars in and lands in the branches of the oaks.
They stamp about like policemen. Thick boots
almost visible in the lacy leaves.
No, those are birds, not boots, clumsy, heavy
leaf-rustlers who tear at twigs and rend
the living bone of the tortured trees and pelt
the lawn below – thup,thup,thup – with acorns.
They give no cry, no coo – a flock of mutes
overhead, deaf mutes perhaps, unhearing
the flail and storm they make stuffing, stuffing
their gullets and sleek bellies with salad fruits.

Through binoculars they are beautiful,
the prettiest pigeons – every feather
each neat little head, white collar, banded tail.
But voracious, gang-despoilers of the treetops
they shake and thrash about in, tiny eyes
riveted upon acorns ah they are gone in a whoosh
wooden rackety twirling noisemakers
and we left hungry in this wingless hush.

1984

The New Bicycle

All the molecules in the house
readjust on its arrival,
make way for its shining presence
its bright dials,
and after it has settled
and the light
has explored its surfaces
– and the night –
they compose themselves again
in another order.

One senses the change at once
without knowing what one senses.
Has somebody cleaned the windows
used different soap
or is there a bowl of flowers
on the mantelpiece? –
for the air makes another shape
it is thinner or denser,
a new design
is invisibly stamped upon it.

How we all adapt ourselves
to the bicycle
aglow in the furnace room,
turquoise where turquoise
has never before been seen,
its chrome gleaming
on gears and pedals,
its spokes glistening.
Lightly resting on the incised
rubber of its airy tires
it has changed us all.

1985

Suffering

Man is made in such a way that he is never so much
attached to anything as he is to his suffering.
GURDJIEFF

Suffering
confers identity. It makes you proud.
The one bird in the family bush. Which other, ever
suffered so? Whose nights, whose days,
a thicket of blades to pass through?
Deeps of tears. Not ever to give it up
this friend whose sword
turns in your heart,
this oh-so-constant clever cove – care-giver
never neglectful, saying yes and yes
to plumed funerary horses, to grey drizzle
falling against the panes of the eyes.

Oh, what without it …? If you turned your back?
Unthinkable, so to reject it, choose instead
meadows flower-starred
or taste, for instance – just for an instant – bread.
The sweet-smelling fields of the earth
dancing
goldenly dancing
in your mouth.

But
suffering is sweeter yet.
That dark embrace – that birthmark,
birthright, even.
Yours forever
ready to be conjured up –
tongue in the sore tooth, fingertip
pressed to the bandaged cut
and mind returning to it over and over.

Best friend, bestower of feeling
status-giver.
Something to suck at like a stone.
One's own. One's owner.
… One's almost lover.

1985

The Gift

'Dried huckleberries,' you said.
'Cram them into your mouth by the handful.'

Like dried bees – not quite stinging.
Rough and tart.
Chewy as a mouthful of springs.

My saliva releases
their ten small bony nutlets.

1986

The Hidden Components

In his palace
the ravaged king
while simple in exile and rags
his falsely dishonoured queen

Naked now in the jungle
safe in a leafy nest
their radiant son and daughter
wards of a giant bird

I see the king's black face
the rigid line of his jaw
He is on stage centre
blind to the hidden components

The queen is harder to see
She is almost transparent   Who
can look through such a window?
The view is a single flower
For some it is white linen

The king is a charred ruin
The queen looks forward and back
Royal castaways, the children
understand the language of birds

More than the sum of their parts
they cannot see one another
the king in his palace the queen
the children safe in the jungle

Cannot foresee that the king
crazed with grief at his loss
wandering deep in the jungle
will discover the royal children

Cannot foresee that the children
a diminutive queen and king
will recognize their father
remember their royal blood

Cannot foresee that the bird
homing into the jungle
will bear on her feathered back
the falsely dishonoured queen

The hidden components await
the possible perfect moment
the invisible conjuror
the triangulation of stars

Meanwhile the king is a ruin
the exiled queen is a window
the children safe in the jungle
converse in the language of birds.

1987

Kaleidoscope

I. A Little Fantasy

> I send you a very well-constructed Kaleidoscope,
> a recently invented Toy.
>
> John Murray to Byron, 1818

So – Murray to Byron in Italy
when B. was falling in love again. In love.
Teresa this time. Guiccioli.
What a gift
to view her through that tube!
Her palms, sand dollars –
pale, symmetrical –
changed with his breathing
into petalled stars.
Four hearts her mouth, then eight,
a single flower
become a bunch
to kiss and kiss and kiss
and kiss a fourth time.
What a field of mouths!

Her navel – curling, complex –
shells and pearls
quadrupling for him
and her soft hair – ah,
the flat, sweet plait of it
beneath the glass –
a private hair brooch
such as ladies wear
pinned to their *peau de soie.*

Byron is breathing heavily
the tube – a lover's perfect toy –
weighting his palm.
'Quite a celestial kaleidoscope.'
But Murray demands more cantos.
(Damn the man!)
Oh, multiple Teresa,
Don Juan calls.

II. A Little Reality

My eye falls headlong
down this slender tube,
its eyebeam glued
to shift and flux and flow.
(Mirrors. A trick with mirrors.)
I cannot
budge from this cylinder.
An octagonal rose
holds me as though I were its stem.
We move
interdependent
paired in serious play
that is not play.
Part of the art
of dance.

Gwendolyn,
your garden of square roots
grows in this circle:
from my pots and pans –
a silver chaparral of leaves & flowers –
the tap's drip dew
upon them – diamonds, stars;
the yellow plastic
of my liquid soap –

a quatrefoil of buttercups –
unfolds
in four-leaf clovers on a field of gold.

Nothing is what it seems.
Through this glass eye
each single thing is other –
all-ways joined
to every other thing.
Familiar here is foreign
fresh and fair
as never-seen-before.
And this kaleidoscope uniting all,
this tube, this conduit optical,
this lens
is magic. Through it – see
(who dares?)
the perfect, all-inclusive metaphor.

1987

Lily on the Patio

It's like a slender person in a pot
as tall as I am in my heels, a presence
perfumed, parasolled, imperious.
Dispassionate. Neuter. Mute.

A budding Beanstalk – but no Jack am I
nor Jill, to climb its spiky leaves to heaven.
And where the sun shines through it who can tell
its colour. Is it green chartreuse? Or yellow?

Swings like a yacht at anchor in some sweet
and imperceptible breeze,
some silken rearrangement of the air
– sleeves of kimonos loose –

to waft its inner essence on us where
in our gross human flesh we stupefy
while silently – a bare brown foot away –
its open-mouthed enamelled trumpets bray.

Silence is where it leads. Its phantom gift –
sheer voicelessness. Those swinging scented shafts
beamed from its lighthouse and oblivious
of noisy all of us

are like neutrinos touching us without our knowing.
Doing who knows what
as they pass through us?
Answer: *Who* knows what.

1988

This Heavy Craft

The wax has melted
but the dream of flight
persists.
I, Icarus, though grounded
in my flesh
have one bright section in me
where a bird
night after starry night
while I'm asleep
unfolds its phantom wings
and practises.

1990

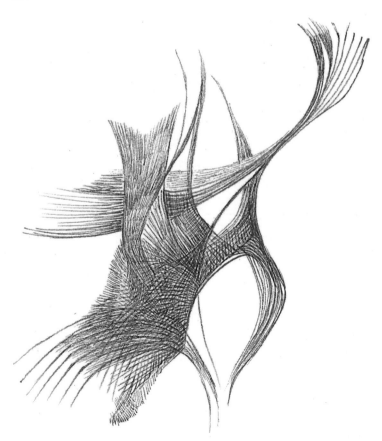

Chinook

Fought in a rush, this war between winter and summer with winter
vanquished – its armour unlocked in a flash, its white flesh melted. But
this is love, not war.

It is fifty below. Look west and you see the chinook arch over the Rockies.
It is a promise – like the rainbow. The voluptuous, warm wind is on its
way. Already the clouds are beginning to spin. The snow will vanish, the
ice thaw. A midwinter miracle.

At night, you toss off your bedclothes, suddenly hot. Your ears are filled
with the rush of that great embracing wind, for it *is* a great embrace as it
fills the night, and you want to run out naked to greet it. The icicles drip
from the eaves. By morning, there will be nothing of winter left. You will
refuse to put on your heavy coat and your mittens.

After the harsh sounds of zero: the crunch, the squeak of heels, of wheels
in packed snow, the groan and grind of ice – how sweet the susurrations
of that warm wind like a flock of birds in flight, and the whole city, in its
beautiful false spring, running with freshets, storm sewers roaring.

1991

The World

It is like a treacle, the world.
I am caught in its golden threads,
a fly in a honey pot.

1991

Conversation

'We were set in the green enamel of Brazil –
you, monumental, an Old Testament prophet, caught
mid-stride and speaking in utterances:
"Thou shalt. Thou shalt not."'

    'But – we were laughing. Have you forgotten?
    I was high – higher than Corcovado on the light
    the colour, the sharp smell of turps
    and the little jewel of a canvas we had made:
    insects, of all things, winged and crawling, bright
    iridescent bodies, hexagonal eyes
    and the absolute stamp of air
    in the gauze of their wings.
    No "shalt". No "shalt not".'

'I was laughing – true. Not up to utterances.
Able only to slosh and slosh my brush
in the paint your Old Testament hand had mixed
with such assurance – additive colour – paint like light,
when under its sudden weight, my hand collapsed.
Each cell grew heavy. My arm fell.

'It was then you put the fire in the canvas,
flame in the wings.
Made little phoenixes of the simple flies.
Spun, on the ball of your foot.'

1991

Address at Simon Fraser (excerpt)

. . . .

But to get back to art, for there my heart is,
there – beyond materiality,
beyond the buy-and-sell, beyond the want
embedded in us, and beyond desire –
resides the magic greed has cancelled out.   .
If we'll but give it time, a work of art
'can rap and knock and enter in our souls'
and re-align us – all our molecules –
to make us whole again. A work of art,
could, 'had we but world enough and time,'
portray for us – all Paradise apart –
'the face (we) had/before the world was made,'
or, to compound the image, vivify
Plato's invisible reality.

But is there time enough? This turning world
we call our home, or *notre pays* – could
become inimical to humankind –
humanunkind as cummings might have said –
in fewer years than I have walked this earth.

So, what is there to tell you? Only this.
'Imagination is the star in man.'
Read *woman*, if you wish. And though we are
trapped in the body of an animal,
we're half angelic, and our angel ear,
which hears the music of the spheres, can hear
the planet's message, dark, admonishing,
as the archaic torso of Apollo
admonished Rilke, 'You must change your life.'

Art and the planet tell us. Change your life.

1991

The End

Not every man knows what he shall sing at the end,
Watching the pier as the ship sails away, or what it will seem like
When he's held by the sea's roar, motionless, there at the end,
Or what he shall hope for once it is clear that he'll never go back.

   The End, MARK STRAND

In the story, you come at last to a high wall.
Some who have scaled it say they were stricken blind
yet lacked a blind man's skills – white cane, dark glasses.
One girl I know clambered up and gazing over
saw the familiar universe reversed
as in a looking glass. But when that world
beckoned to her complicitously, she turned
from its mirror image as if burned –
wordless, without music, without sound.
Not every man knows what he shall sing at the end.

And one, composed of light, came back he said
to tell me it was not *not* everlasting there
as once he had assumed, that I was right.
Was he not proof? 'Touch me,' he said. I touched
and he was flesh, blood, hair – even as before.
It was the purest heartbreak.
'Tell me …' I said. Bemused, he shook his head.
'It's personal. When your turn comes you'll know.
Till then you cannot guess what you will think
watching the pier as the ship sails away, or what it will seem like,

'nor can I possibly tell you.' His voice was fading
and beneath the palms of my hands he suddenly vanished
as if he had never been – except for two things:
in the darkness I could see, and I was staring
at my fingers where they had touched him, staring
at my mouth, new, where he had kissed it; and
it was clear to me now there was nothing to fear
and no reason for anyone, here or anywhere
to suppose he will be drowned
when he's held by the sea's roar, motionless, there at the end.

For he belongs to the sea – we all do. We are part of its swell.
And only the shoreline grounds us. Yet we stand
hands tied, deluded, seemingly earthbound
imagining we belong to the land
which is only a way – station, after all.
We are the sea's, and as such we are at its beck.
We are the water within the wave and the wave's form.
And little will man – or woman, come to that –
know what he shall dream when drawn by the sea's wrack
or what he shall hope for once it is clear that he'll never go back.

1993

Love's Pavilion

Though they go mad they shall be sane,
Though they sink through the sea they shall rise again;
Though lovers be lost love shall not;
And death shall have no dominion.

And Death Shall Have No Dominion, DYLAN THOMAS

Tell me the truth. How does it end?
Who will untangle their matted hair?
Shine in the dark hole of their sleep?
Though they rattle the stones in their broken brains,
in their thicket of words who will find a way,
discover a path through unmapped terrain?
When will the unpretentious air
fall like rain on the ache of their skin?
What is the price they pay for pain?

Though they go mad they shall be sane.

What is the hope for those who drown?
Pickled in brine? Stripped to the bone?
Who will they meet in deep sea lanes?
Or, when they find themselves alone,
too far up or too far down
beyond the reach of hell or heaven
how will they speak who have no tongue?
Who will they be when their bones are gone?
Bodiless, are they anyone?

Though they sink through the sea they shall rise again.

And what of the heart like an empty cup;
heart like a drum; red blood – white?
How can they twin when their love has gone?
How can they live when their love has died?
When the reins to their chariot have been cut?
What of the plot and counterplot
families devise to keep apart
Romeo from Juliet?
And what of the lovers of Camelot?

Though lovers be lost love shall not.

Love shall not. O, love shall not.
Engrave it in stone. Carve it in rock.
This is the subtext of all art,
the wind in the wings of the Paraclete.
With the Lord of the Dance we shall form a ring
and there in love's pavilion
hand in hand we shall say Amen
and we shall dance and we shall sing
with Love, with Love for companion.

And death shall have no dominion.

1993

Planet Earth

It has to be spread out, the skin of this planet,
has to be ironed, the sea in its whiteness;
and the hands keep on moving,
smoothing the holy surfaces.

In Praise of Ironing, PABLO NERUDA

It has to be loved the way a laundress loves her linens,
the way she moves her hands caressing the fine muslins
knowing their warp and woof,
like a lover coaxing, or a mother praising.
It has to be loved as if it were embroidered
with flowers and birds and two joined hearts upon it.
It has to be stretched and stroked.
It has to be celebrated.
O this great beloved world and all the creatures in it.
It has to be spread out, the skin of this planet.

The trees must be washed, and the grasses and mosses.
They have to be polished as if made of green brass.
The rivers and little streams with their hidden cresses
and pale-coloured pebbles
and their fool's gold
must be washed and starched or shined into brightness,
the sheets of lake water
smoothed with the hand
and the foam of the oceans pressed into neatness.
It has to be ironed, the sea in its whiteness

and pleated and goffered, the flower-blue sea
the protean, wine-dark, grey, green, sea
with its metres of satin and bolts of brocade.
And sky – such an O! overhead – night and day
must be burnished and rubbed
by hands that are loving
so the blue blazons forth
and the stars keep on shining
within and above
and the hands keep on moving.

It has to be made bright, the skin of this planet
till it shines in the sun like gold leaf.
Archangels then will attend to its metals
and polish the rods of its rain.
Seraphim will stop singing hosannas
to shower it with blessings and blisses and praises
and, newly in love,
we must draw it and paint it
our pencils and brushes and loving caresses
smoothing the holy surfaces.

1993

Presences

Extraordinary presences, the sunlight seeming
to light them from within, tall alabaster
amphoras with flames inside them
motionless within the grove, their shadows
like chlorophyll, like leaves, like water
slipping from a silver jug, reflecting
grasses, the long pliant stalks of willows.
And when they turned to us, their brightness spilled
over our skin and hair and, like a blessing,
there they were as our guests, accepted and accepting.

Only our golden selves went forth to greet them
that part of us which receiving blows
feels neither pain nor grief, the part that senses
joy in a higher register and moves
through a country of continuous light
shed by the one god, by the sun god, Aten –
moves as Nefertiti and her daughters
moved through their city of continuous light
in the pharaonic kingdom of Aknaten.
So we moved, and they, in a formal pattern.

Our feet barely touched the earth, and memory
erased at birth, but gradually reassembling
coalesced and formed a whole, as single birds
gathering for migration form a flock.
And some new incandescence in our heads
led us from the shadows to the sparkle
of Aten-light where we at last remembered
the arc of our lives, the distant stars we came from
and walked – O joy, O very miracle! –
along the empty alley, into the box circle.

And so to the maze with its forking paths which seen
from above, entire, was like a map –
or like a rose unfolding, a yellow rose,
opening in the unreflecting air –
the green of its leaves
the Garden before the fall,
every atom accurately aligned,
and there we walked in youthful innocence
until we came at last – new-born, royal –
to look down into the drained pool.

1993

Autumn

Whoever has no house now will never have one.
Whoever is alone will stay alone
Will sit, read, write long letters through the evening
And wander on the boulevards, up and down ...

       Autumn Day, RAINER MARIA RILKE

Its stain is everywhere.
The sharpening air
of late afternoon
is now the colour of tea.
Once-glycerined green leaves
burned by a summer sun
are brittle and ochre.
Night enters day like a thief.
And children fear that the beautiful daylight has gone.
Whoever has no house now will never have one.

It is the best and the worst time.
Around a fire, everyone laughing,
brocaded curtains drawn,
nowhere – anywhere – is more safe than here.
The whole world is a cup
one could hold in one's hand like a stone
warmed by that same summer sun.
But the dead or the near dead
are now all knucklebone.
Whoever is alone will stay alone.

Nothing to do. Nothing to really do.
Toast and tea are nothing.
Kettle boils dry.
Shut the night out or let it in,
it is a cat on the wrong side of the door
whichever side it is on. A black thing
with its implacable face.
To avoid it you
will tell yourself you are something,
will sit, read, write long letters through the evening.

Even though there is bounty, a full harvest
that sharp sweetness in the tea-stained air
is reserved for those who have made a straw
fine as a hair to suck it through –
fine as a golden hair.
Wearing a smile or a frown
God's face is always there.
It is up to you
if you take your wintry restlessness into the town
and wander on the boulevards, up and down.

1993

The Gold Sun

Trace the gold sun about the whitened sky
Without evasion by a single metaphor.
Look at it in its essential barrenness
And say this, this is the centre that I seek.

    Credences of Summer, WALLACE STEVENS

Sky whitened by a snow on which no swan
is visible, and no least feather falling
could possibly or impossibly be seen,
sky whitened like the blank page of a book,
no letters forming into words unless
written in paleness – a pallidity
faint as the little rising moons on nails –
and so, forgettable and so, forgot.
Blue eyes dark as lapis lazuli
trace the gold sun about the whitened sky.

You'll see the thing itself no matter what.
Though it may blind you, what else will suffice?
To smoke a glass or use a periscope
will give you other than the very thing,
or more, or elements too various.
So let the fabulous photographer
catch Phaeton in his lens and think he is
the thing itself, not knowing all the else
he is become. But you will see it clear
without evasion by a single metaphor.

How strip the sun of all comparisons?
That spinning coin – moving, yet at rest
in its outflinging course across the great
parabola of space – is Phoebus,
sovereign: heroic principle,
the heat and light of us. And gold – no less
a metaphor than sun – is not the least
less multiple and married. Therefore how
rid the gold sun of all its otherness?
Look at it in its essential barrenness.

Make a prime number of it, pure, and know
it indivisible and hold it so
in the white sky behind your lapis eyes.
Push aside everything that isn't sun
the way a sculptor works his stone,
the way a mystic masters the mystique
of making more by focusing on one
until at length, all images are gone
except the sun, the thing itself, deific,
and say this, this is the centre that I seek.

1993

Poor Bird

... looking for something, something, something.
Poor bird, he is obsessed!
The millions of grains are black, white, tan, and gray,
mixed with quartz grains, rose and amethyst.

Sandpiper, ELIZABETH BISHOP

From birth, from the first astonishing moment
when he pecked his way out of the shell, pure fluff,
he was looking for something – warmth, food, love
or light, or darkness – we are all the same stuff,
all have the same needs: to be one of the flock
or to stand apart, a singular fledgling.
So the search began – the endless search
that leads him onward – a vocation
year in, year out, morning to evening
looking for something, something, something.

Nothing will stop him. Although distracted
by nest-building, eggs, high winds, high tides
and too short a lifespan for him to plan
an intelligent search – still, on he goes
with his delicate legs and spillikin feet
and the wish to know what he's almost guessed.
Can't leave it alone, that stretch of sand.
Thinks himself Seurat (pointilliste)
or a molecular physicist.
Poor bird, he is obsessed!

And just because he has not yet found
what he doesn't know he is searching for
is not a sign he's off the track.
His track is the sedge, the sand, the suck
of the undertow, the line of shells.
Nor would he have it another way.
And yet – the nag – is there something else?
Something more, perhaps, or something less.
And though he examine them, day after day
the millions of grains are black, white, tan, and gray.

But occasionally, when he least expects it,
in the glass of a wave a painted fish
like a work of art across his sight
reminds him of something he doesn't know
that he has been seeking his whole long life –
something that may not even exist!
Poor bird, indeed! Poor dazed creature!
Yet when his eye is sharp and sideways seeing
oh, *then* the quotidian unexceptional sand is
mixed with quartz grains, rose and amethyst.

1993

Hologram

All that morning we looked at the citadel from every angle.
We began from the side in the shadow, where the sea,
Green without brilliance, – breast of a slain peacock,
Received us like time that has no break in it.

    The King of Asine, GEORGE SEFERIS

It was astonishing, larger by far than we could imagine,
larger than sight itself but still we strained to see it.
It was Kafka's castle in a dream of wonder,
nightmare transmuted, black become golden,
buttresses disappearing in the cloud and azure:
a new geometry of interlocking octangles
and we, watching it, interlocked in a strange dimension –
that neither your heart nor mine could have invented –
of multiple images, complex as angels.
All that morning we looked at the citadel from every angle.

But that was later, after we had made the passage
from the faint light of morning star and pale moon
to unscrupulous noonday with its major chords –
battalions marching across an Escher landscape.
For us, at first, there was no hint of clarity,
no hint of anything that wasn't misty –
synaesthetic layers and lengths of space-time
leading us inward, downward, upward, as –
from all directions at once – observing closely,
we began from the side in the shadow and the sea.

Brave of us to begin in darkness. Or was it wisdom
that made us so prepare ourselves for that radiance
little by little? A Jurassic age must pass before even colour
could enter the scene – dawn's greys being so infinite
and infinitely subtle – transparencies, opacities.
And then we sensed it together – the tremulous foreshock
of what lay ahead: what could not be imagined,
possibly not even dreamed, a new range of experience.
And – unbelievably – what revealed itself as earthquake
was green, without brilliance, breast of a slain peacock.

But to the cones of our eyes that green was shining
and pierced us like a spear. (When joy is great enough
how distinguish it from pain?) And after the fugal greys
and the near-invisible shafts of no-colour that had stained us,
how could our eyes adjust to so full a spectrum?
And yet in a flash, from infra-red to ultra-violet,
we saw the hologram glittering above us
glistening in air we could suddenly enter like swallows
as the whole citadel, rainbowed, immediate,
received us like time that has no break in it.

1994

The Castle

It is the stress that holds the structure up.
Birds in its turrets tilt it not at all.
Balance is inner, centred in the keep.

Marble and timber crumble as we sleep.
Centuries of creeper cannot sustain a wall.
It is the stress that holds the structure up.

Lovers in spirals, turning in the deep
well of their rapture, dizzyingly recall
balance is inner, centred in the keep.

Patients, post-crisis, feel the fever drop.
The pendulum begins its swing from ill to well.
It is the stress that holds the structure up.

Whoever – dreaming – dances a tightrope
knows where is balance, just before the fall!
Balance is inner, centred in the keep.

Insomnia, pain and trouble have a stop
definitive, sudden, at the terminal.
It was the stress that held the structure up.
But balance is inner, centred in the keep.

1996

Funeral Mass

In his blackest suit
the father carries the coffin

It is light as a box of kleenex
He carries it in one hand

It is white and gold
A jewel box

Their baby is in it

In the unconscionable weather
the father sweats and weeps

The mother leans
on the arms of two women friends

By the sacred light of the church
they are pale as gristle

The priests talk Latin
change their elaborate clothes

their mitres, copes
their stoles embroidered by nuns

Impervious to grief
their sole intention

is the intricate ritual
of returning a soul to God

this sinless homunculus
this tiny seed

1996

The Hidden Room

I have been coming here since I was born
never at my will
only when it permits me

Like the Bodleian like the Web
like Borges' aleph
it embodies all

It is in a house
deeply hidden in my head
It is mine and notmine

yet if I seek it
it recedes
down corridors of ether

Each single version
is like and unlike
all the others

a hidden place
in cellar or attic
matrix of evil and good

a room
disguised as a non-room
a secret space

I am showing it to you
fearful you may not
guess its importance

that you will see only
a lumber room
a child's bolt-hole

Will not know it as prism
a magic square
the number nine

1996

Like a Cruise Ship

It is like a cruise ship bursting into flower
or a municipal building intricately blooming.
And its myriad miniature petals blink as I pass.

Each year it grows more outrageous, spreads itself
unpruned, untended, a vegetable amphitheatre
with pizzicato blossoms pinking the air.

Oh, tree! I say as I whizz past, bowing. I bow. I whizz
powered by some high-octane fumeless fuel
that spring has invented. Oh, tree! I say. *Tree. Tree!*

And the word is new – *another* of spring's inventions.
Newer than *biots* or *quarks* or *nanoseconds*.

1996

Request to the Alchemist

I am a tin whistle
Blow through me
Blow through me
And make my tin
     Gold

1996

But We Rhyme in Heaven

For Dorothy Livesay – d. 1996

It is true. We shall. We do.
But earth is a briar patch –
one we never get through.
The moment we meet
tangles and snares spring up
on the asphalt street.
At airports and theatres
magnets pull us together
and we go for each other.

It is so irrational.
What is the bloody bone
we struggle and fight for?
Not my bone. Not hers.
An astrological quirk?
Or grit in the oil of the works
that set us in motion – some
meddlesome tamperer's mischief?
No part of us.

But her anguished, defiant phrase –
'we rhyme in heaven!'
is like a balloon
that carries our anger up
to a rarefied air
where rancour is blown away,
and remedial stars appear,
and Venus is kissing the moon
as the Spanish say.

1997

Alphabetical (excerpt)

. . . .

As a child I was wakened
taken from my tent
to look at the velvet
vastness of the night.

I had never seen my parents' eyes
so glistening,
such wonder on their faces
like the look of love
they gave me in the mornings.

Standing between them
barefoot on the prairie
I looked deeper and deeper in.

Eternity rushed past.

*

We set forth
on this long journey
sleeping.

How waken
when
we think we are awake?

Each least xx, xy
its mother's marvel
moving from school
to marriage
then to children –
and what more real
and wide awake than children?

So dynasties begin
and we their founders.

Surely
we could not do *this*
in our sleep.

*

Arithmetic bored me –
I thought it a tool for housewives –
but in my teens
the tidy
algebraic knot
the perfect puzzle
the code of x plus y
the beautiful clean
equilibrium of equations
fired me.
I was a sudden mathematician.

This love was purer
than my passion for pig Latin
and those difficult linguistic
'pigs' that followed.

Should I, instead, have been
a cipher clerk?

*

On the computer keyboard
Yes and No
hide behind Y and N.
A binary choice.

No equivalent
for de Bono's munificent *po* –
poetry, possibility, the prefix *poly* –
a chance
to see around corners
or enter
the scale between extremes.
To fly – perhaps.

Sooner rather than later
we also learn
that lower case l is not the number one.
Upper case O is never zero.

Zero is zero.

*

I have circled zero
over and over
in love with the aperture
where the face of light
might appear.

With Euclid's compass
I draw beautiful circles.
I trace man-hole covers, ride Ferris wheels,
wear rings on my fingers –
all are zero.
A port-hole awaiting that luminous face.

How visualize nothingness –
rare gift from Arabia –
absence of all magnitude?

And – afterwards?

How anticipate
afterwards?

1998

Cosmologies

I

Imagine eight universes – parallel.
The first is the one in which you said, 'I love you.'
I, weak with desire, wanted only your mouth.
In the others even the alphabet is different.

The first is the one in which you said, 'I love you.'
What, I ask, was heard in the other seven?
In the others even the alphabet is different
and we, cut off from higher frequencies.

What, I ask, was heard in the other seven?
The first is literal, material, flesh –
and we, cut off from higher frequencies,
blind inhabitants of a diving-bell.

The first is literal, material, flesh –
low C of an ascending scale.
Blind inhabitants of a diving-bell,
a leaf obliterates Mount Everest.

Low C of an ascending scale
as ordered as the colours of the rainbow.
A leaf obliterates Mount Everest.
Mouth, for me, the obliterating leaf.

As ordered as the colours of the rainbow,
the tonic sol-fa – its eight syllables.
Mouth, for me, the obliterating leaf –
your mouth, saying the words, 'I love you.'

The tonic sol-fa – its eight syllables.
I, weak with desire, wanted only your mouth,
your mouth, saying the words, 'I love you.'
Imagine eight universes – parallel.

II

The second universe – is it like the first? –
grass, sky, blossoming trees in springtime,
rain, beloved waters, rivers, lakes,
during the dark months, rumour has it, snow.

Grass, sky, blossoming trees in springtime –
nature ostensibly the same as here.
During the dark months, rumour has it, snow
but temperate or not, we cannot know.

Nature ostensibly the same as here.
The colours slightly altered. The air softer.
But temperate or not, we cannot know
which is the prototype, and which the copy.

The colours slightly altered? The air softer?
Changes too subtle for our grosser senses.
Which is the prototype, and which the copy?
Paler or darker – how can we compare?

Changes too subtle for our grosser senses.
Geometry unreliable; and colours
paler or darker – how can we compare?
And do I love you less or love you more?

Geometry unreliable and colours.
Who are we in the second universe?
And do I love you less or love you more?
Our antic brains and fragile nervous systems.

Who are we in the second universe?
– Rain, beloved waters, rivers, lakes,
our antic brains and fragile nervous systems –
the second universe – is it like the first?

III

Now it is guesswork. Speculation fails.
The third is indecipherable, obscure.
Its stars, its solar systems, and its tao
are consummate, regardless of my view.

The third is indecipherable, obscure,
the fourth, the fifth, the entirety overhead
are consummate, regardless of my view.
My head is huge, an enlarged body part.

The fourth, the fifth, the entirety overhead
blow me away. I am a dandelion clock –
my head is huge, an enlarged body part,
free floating in an altered consciousness.

Blow me away, I am a dandelion clock
telling unreliable time at every breath
free floating in an altered consciousness –
in those not-to-be-imagined cosmoses.

Telling unreliable time at every breath
I become alpha, minus height and weight
in those not-to-be-imagined cosmoses.
Star-shine is far more wondrous than my light.

I become alpha. Minus height and weight.
Body amorphous – elbow, knee and ear.
Star-shine is far more wondrous than my light
in which I unknow all that I have known.

Body amorphous – elbow, knee and ear –
its stars, its solar systems and its tao
in which I unknow all that I have known.
Now it is guesswork. Speculation fails.

1998

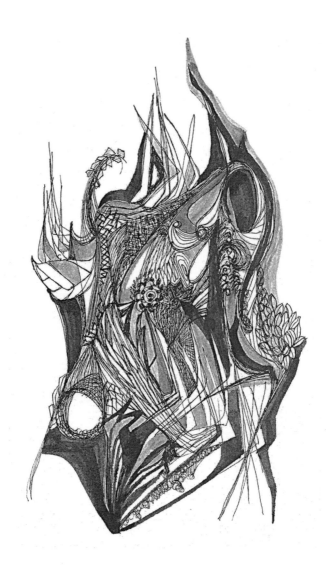

Even Lucifer

Even Lucifer wears mourning today
Black Luggage
Black Luggage
For a good man gone in a puff of smoke

1999

Poem Canzonic with love to A M K

The sky is prussian blue, no, indigo
with just the merest hint of *ultramar.*
I am not painting it, so what care I?
And yet, I do care, deeply, as if life
depended on my skill to mix that blue.
Not my life only – your life, damn it! – *our*
whole planetary life:
the life of beetle, and ichneumon fly
plankton, crustacean, elk and polar bear
the delicate veined leaf
that blows against an enigmatic sky.

It is the writer's duty to describe
freely, exactly. Nothing less will do.
Just as the painter must, from two make three
or conjure light, build pigments layer on layer
to form an artefact, so I must probe
with measuring mind and eye to mix a blue
mainly composed of air.
What is my purpose? This I cannot say
unless, that I may somehow, anyhow
chronicle and compare
each least nuance and inconsistency.

This is the poem Abraham Moses Klein
wrote better, earlier, so why should I
write it again in this so difficult form?
His was a *tour de force,* a *cri de coeur.*
Mine is an urgent need to recombine
pigments and words, and so to rectify
and possibly restore
some lost arcanum from my past, some Om
secure, I thought, until I lost the key
or it lost me; before
birth intervened and – like a chloroform –

erased my archive, made me start again.
Vestigial memory only – vaguest dream
looming through mists, or like St. Elmo's fire
high in the riggings and phantasmal masts,
my one-eyed guide to seeing further in
or further out, to up-or-down the stream
of unremembered pasts –
might show me how to mix and how to name
that blue that is not cobalt or sapphire,
or fugitive, or fast;
and find the key that opens Here – and There.

2002

Ah, by the Golden Lilies

... ah by the golden lilies,
the tepid, golden water,
the yellow butterflies
over the yellow roses ...

Yellow Spring, JUAN RAMÓN JIMÉNEZ

Jiménez, but for the roses
you paint a Rio garden
where every golden morning
the golden sunlight spills
on my Brazilian breakfast –
coffee like bitter aloes
strawberry-fleshed papayas
the sensuous persimmon ...
My young head full of follies
ah, by the golden lilies.

Beneath the cassia boughs
where fallen yellow blossoms
reflect a mirror image
I barefoot in the petals
trample a yellow world
while small canaries flutter
over the lotus pond.
I trail my golden fingers –
for I am Midas' daughter –
in the tepid, golden water.

My blue and gold macaw
laughs his demented laughter
dilates his golden pupils –
a golden spider spins
a spangled golden web
for beauty-loving flies.
Above the cassia branches –
the cassia-colored sun.
Above the yellow lilies –
the yellow butterflies.

Jiménez, I am freed
by all this golden clangour.
Jiménez, your roses
denote a falling sound
a sound that will not rhyme
with *sambas jocosos*
macumba, feijoada
Bahían *vatapá.*
A different sun disposes
over the yellow roses.

2002

The Blue Guitar

They said, 'You have a blue guitar,
You do not play things as they are.'
The man replied, 'Things as they are
are changed upon the blue guitar.'

The Blue Guitar, WALLACE STEVENS

I do my best to tell it true
a thing exceeding hard to do
or tell it slant as Emily
advises in her poetry,
and, colour blind, how can I know
if green is blue or cinnabar.
Find me a colour chart that I
can check against a summer sky.
My eye is on a distant star.
They said, 'You have a blue guitar.'

'I have,' the man replied, 'it's true.
The instrument I strum is blue
I strum my joy, I strum my pain
I strum the sun, I strum the rain.
But tell me, what is that to you?
You see things as you think they are.
Remove the mote within your ear
then talk to me of what you hear.'
They said, 'Go smoke a blue cigar!
You do not play things as they are.'

'Things as they are? Above? Below?
In hell or heaven? Fast or slow …?'
They silenced him. 'It's not about
philosophy, so cut it out.
We want the truth and not what you
are playing on the blue guitar.
So start again and play it straight
don't improvise, prevaricate.
Just play things as they really are.'
The man replied, 'Things as they are

are not the same as things that were
or will be in another year.
The literal is rarely true
for truth is old and truth is new
and faceted – a metaphor
for something higher than we are.
I play the truth of Everyman
I play the truth as best I can.
The things I play are better far
when changed upon the blue guitar.'

2002

Green, How Much I Want You Green

Green, how much I want you green.
Great stars of white frost
come with the fish of darkness
that opens the road of dawn.

Somnambular Ballad, FEDERICO GARCÍA LORCA

Landscape of crystals
rock salt and icebergs
white trees, white grasses,
hills forged from pale metals
padlock and freeze me
in the Pleistocene.
See my skin wither
heart become brittle
cast as the Snow Queen.
Green, how much I want you green.

Green oak, green ilex
green weeping willow
green grass and green clover
all my lost youth.
Come before springtime
before the brown locust
come like the rain
that blows in the night
and melts to fine dust
great stars of white frost.

Water, sweet water
chortling, running
the chinooks of my childhood
warm wind, the ripple
of icicles dripping
from my frozen palace.
How sweet the water
moonstones and vodka
poured from a chalice
with the fish of darkness.

Come water, come springtime
come my green lover
with a whistle of grass
to call me to clover.
A key for my lock
small flowers for my crown.
The Ice Age is over,
green moss and green lichen
will paint a green lawn
that opens the road of dawn.

2002

Hand Luggage (excerpt)

Calgary. The twenties. Cold and the sweet
melt of chinooks. A musical weather.
World rippling and running. World
watery with flutes. And woodwinds.
The wonder of water in that icy world.
The magic of melt. And the grief of it. Tears –
heart's hurt? heart's help?

This was the wilderness: western Canada.
Tomahawk country – teepees, coyotes,
cayuses, lariats. The land that Ontario
looked down its nose at. Nevertheless
we thought it civilized. Civilized? Semi.

Remittance men, ranchers – friends of my family –
public school failures, penniless outcasts,
bigoted bachelors with British accents.
But in my classroom, Canadian voices –
hard r's and flat a's, a prairie language –
were teaching me tolerance, telling me something.
This vocal chasm divided my childhood.
Talking across it, a tightrope talker,
corrected at home, corrected in classrooms:
wawteh, wadder – the wryness of words!

Such my preparation for a life of paradox –
a borderland being, barely belonging,
one on the outskirts, over the perimeter.

. . . .

Though sickness and death take their terrible toll
and they did and they do – one's astonishing heart
almost sings through its grief like a bird – water bird –
in the wind and the waves of some vast salty sea.
Explain it? I can't. But it's true I'm in love
with some point beyond sight, with some singular star
for which words won't suffice, which reduce it, in fact.
Head on it's invisible, if I should look
with my cones, not my rods, it would vanish – expunged;
if I glance to the side, through my rods, then the star
shines as brightly as Venus. Which truth is *the* Truth?

*

Nero fiddled. And fiddled. What else could he do?

2003–05

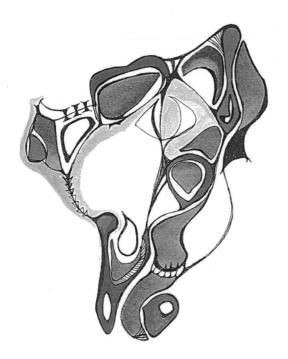

My Chosen Landscape

I am a continent, a violated geography.
Yet still I journey to this naked country,
to seek a form which dances in the sand.
This is my chosen landscape.

     Finally Left in the Landscape, GWENDOLYN MACEWEN

Sand dunes, interminable deserts, burning winds
the night temperatures bitter, a land of grit;
and floating above me stars as violent
as fire balloons, tactile and brilliant.
The all-enveloping sky, a cloak of soot.
This is my story, my brief biography.
The sum total of my experience. I travel –
a compass useless in my useless hand –
through a sandscape, a singular topography.
I am a continent, a violated geography.

Restless in all this emptiness, I seek
a fellow traveller, search for a sign –
a secret handshake, a phrase, some unusual colour
like periwinkle, for instance, or bright citrine,
but the monotony of sand persists
and nothing improbable finds entry
into the appalling platitudes of speech –
the *lingua franca* of everyone I meet –
in this land devoid of flags and pageantry.
Yet still I journey to this naked country,

for something in its nakedness has a beauty
so pure it is as if I thrust a knife
into my immaculate flesh and drew it forth
without a drop of blood being spilled. It is
abstract and invisible as air
this empty geometry, this ampersand
upon ampersand that leads me on
as if I were zero or the minus sign,
through 'and' and 'and' and 'and',
to seek a form which dances in the sand.

But nothing formal dances. Only the wind
blows – unchoreographed – a floating ghost
across the dunes. The sand molecular,
airborne and free, is faint with the scent
of absolute dryness, a small mineral smell.
And this almost scentlessness, this shape without shape
is a violated country, one in which
I am both exile and inhabitant
and though I would escape
this is my chosen landscape.

2006

Coal and Roses – A Triple Glosa

Everything is plundered, betrayed, sold,
Death's great black wing scrapes the air,
Misery gnaws to the bone.
Why then do we not despair?

      Everything is Plundered ..., ANNA AKHMATOVA

I.
I read the papers with my morning coffee.
Only the horoscope columns offer hope.
We sell our birthright piecemeal to our neighbour.
Our natural resources are going, going, gone –
our oil, our gas, our water, clear-cut forests.
We dynamite glaciers in our greed for gold.
Polar bears, seeking ice floes, swim and drown.
The pillars of our society are felons.
To those of us who knew a more innocent world,
everything is plundered, betrayed, sold.

How many children, this week, shot their mothers?
How many mothers drowned their two-year-olds?
Car bombs account for many, cluster bombs.
Madmen shoot up classrooms, shoot themselves.
This week's body bags again outnumber
the body bags of last week. Who can bear
those plastic-wrapped, young, beautiful, rigid corpses
shipped to their grieving girlfriends, pregnant wives?
My armband weeps, I weep, and everywhere
death's great black wing scrapes the air.

Street people line the sidewalks, homeless people,
hands out, begging – the unemployable
with all hope gone. Go on, take a dare –
stare in those vacant eyes that gaze on nothing
but heartache, hunger, unimaginable despair.
His Honour, the Mayor of our bustling town,
complains they are ruining the tourist business,
their visibility – a mortal sin
against the holy dollar. O God, where have you gone?
Misery gnaws to the bone.

Prices go up and up. The rich are richer.
La dolce vita in every household, gourmet fare
ordered from gourmet takeouts. The new kitchen,
now an appliance showcase, gadgets galore,
high tech, electric. Hydro cuts a bagel!
Alarm systems only increase our fear.
What are we locking out? our kids on crack?
thieves with firearms? the all-enveloping dark?
Terrorism brandishes weapons everywhere.
Why then do we not despair?

By day, from the surrounding woods,
cherries blow summer into town;
at night the deep transparent skies
glitter with new galaxies

    Everything is Plundered …

II.
Perhaps the crocus, with its furry presence
pushing toward the sunlight through the snow
offers us hope that the whole world is waking
and making music. Tulips, daffodils
narcissus, jonquils, hyacinths, all the bulbs
that paint the air and cram the flowerbeds
sweet-talk us into festival and folly.
By night, a fragrant vegetable scent
hovers above the new thin summer bedspreads.
By day, from the surrounding woods

bird calls sound. Nest building is beginning.
Fledglings will hatch and fly. The seasons turn
in ordered, immemorial procession.
Despite excessive rains, power cuts and winds
of hurricane proportions – this is spring:
the longed-for after-winter everyone
was dreaming during those dark months of waiting –
an alternate reality, a bright wing.
And suddenly the grass is overgrown,
cherries blow summer into town

and kids wear shorts and singlets, and pale girls
search out last year's sandals, part their hair
the other side perhaps, pubescent boys
buy after-shave and condoms. Everywhere
there is a shine, rain glistens, threads of sun
are weaving multicoloured tapestries,
spiders spin webs, even the dung beetle
dreams his own small wonderful dream of heaven.
By day the universe is like a kiss,
at night the deep transparent skies

carry us upwards, outwards, into space.
Lie on your back on cooling grass and stare.
Like Zeus, the Perseids shower us with their gold,
and 'Look!' we cry and 'Look!' They come so close
they almost touch us and their pale, cold fire
links us with heaven and the Pleiades.
Flesh is forgotten; gone the hoof and horn,
the claw, the canine teeth, the bitter blood
as overhead the deepening darknesses
glitter with new galaxies.

And the miraculous comes so close
to the ruined, dirty houses –
something not known to anyone at all
but wild in our breast for centuries.

      Everything is Plundered ...

III.
There is a place, not here, not there. No dream
nor opiate can conjure it – it is
not heaven, though heavenly – it is its own
element – not sea, not earth, not air,
nothing approximate, nor half way matched,
where other laws prevail. It honours those
who enter it like water, without wish
vainglorious or trivial – a gift
from realms of outer unimagined space.
And the miraculous comes so close

it alters us. It is as if a beam
embraced us and transformed our molecules
and merged us with some cosmological
and fractal universe we never dreamed,
more vast than any thought we had of love
divine or secular, a synthesis
of right and wrong, of midday, midnight, dawn,
of poverty and wealth, sackcloth and silk.
A gift of coal and roses
to the ruined, dirty houses

and to their opposites – the shining palaces
floating above in towers of cumulus –
that take on size the way a child's balloon
can fill with breath, or perfume scent a room.
This beam – not tenuous or crystalline,
minus proportions, neither large nor small –
is all-encompassing, a kind of womb,
a 'heaven-haven' and improbable,
some entity beyond recall.
Something not known to anyone at all.

And yet it is our heartbeat, intimate
and human. Here, my wrist – its pulse
is yours for the taking, yet it is not yours.
We share a heartbeat, share lub-dub, lub-dub.
All races, genders, share that little drum
and share its Drummer and its mysteries.
This quiet clock, unnoticed day by day,
our ghost attendant, is invisible,
untouchable, perhaps sublunary.
But wild in our breast for centuries.

2006

Your Slightest Look

your slightest look easily will unclose me
though I have closed myself as fingers,
you open always petal by petal myself as Spring opens
(touching skillfully, mysteriously) her first rose

      somewhere I have never traveled, gladly beyond, E. E. CUMMINGS

Together in a restaurant, at a party,
where I have never travelled gladly –
or in the evening, listening to disasters
on national newscasts hourly and/or reading
scaremongering headlines in the evening paper,
arguing over politics and/or poetry
whatever we are doing, doing daily
moderately attentive, inattentive –
if I should glance your way, observing closely,
your slightest look easily will unclose me.

No matter if I sleep, my dream will see you
looking my way, the curious gaze you give me
bringing you to me bringing us both together
as if I were between you, you between me
in a sweet lovers' bow knot, and/or double,
our twoness only one, our twice-times single
as two eyes in a face, two hands together,
as two halves of a peach, and/or an apple.
I swear that – this my love song, I the singer –
though I have closed myself as fingers

are folded in a sleeping fist, and lazy,
my song continues in unspoken ways –
in images and/or surrealist music
in landscape, seascape, skyscape and/or air
until you break it with your laser eye's
accurate and/or unerring focus.
And I awaken with luxurious slowness
still soft from Morpheus – a drowsy flower
(yours for the picking, yet unpicked, and/or unbroken)
you open always petal by petal myself as Spring opens

crocus and aconite. A slow uncurling
from bud to brightest full-face turned to heaven.
I do not know the chemistry of bodies
yet know no other hands, and/or no lips,
which can so capably and quite uncurl me
outward, you-ward, into your embrace.
You are the world's blue skies and/or its rain
you are sweet-scented blossoms in a fervour
but most of all you are a summer breeze
(touching skillfully, mysteriously) her first rose.

2007

How to Write a Poem

This poem is concerned with language on a very plain level.
Look at it talking to you. You look out a window
Or pretend to fidget. You have it but you don't have it.
You miss it, it misses you. You miss each other.

　　　Paradoxes and Oxymorons, JOHN ASHBERY

It is raining and you've decided you are going to write a poem.
What else is there to do besides phoning your mother?
And you don't feel like it not because you don't like your mother
in actual fact you love her and phone very often
but right now you have decided you are going to write a poem
and this poem will be a poem that you hope will be special.
Nothing symbolic or complicated, simple words, and language
a child could understand, but not a poem for children
with a moral and the struggle of good over evil.
This poem is concerned with language on a very plain level.

You are ready to begin. You have sharpened your pencil
the paper is lined in blue and is quite a bright yellow.
Listen to the poem talk, hear the words come together
and write them slowly and clearly so you can read them later.
This is the easy part, like taking dictation.
You must be deaf to long words like 'crescendo', 'diminuendo',
or cross them out if they surface, they are not for this poem,
and avoid scientific terms, botanical names or medical,
and a musical vocabulary – 'accelerando', 'glissando'.
Look at it talking to you. You look out a window

to avoid the poem's glance, turn away, embarrassed
by the poem and the fact that you're not fully attentive.
You are thinking of the rain that is beating with fury
against the dirty glass. You are thinking about everything
except the poem – about the gutters overflowing,
and is the cat in? But the poem begs you to give it
more than you are giving. The poem is expecting
your total attention. When it talks, you must listen.
Don't look abstracted – (O scribe, you must love it) –
or pretend to fidget. You have it but you don't have it.

It's not easy to focus. Perhaps the plain language
is what makes it so difficult. This poem's elusive –
a flirt, comes and goes, takes back what was given.
(There are phrases that describe it but you don't want to use them.)
Now the wind has come up and the cedars are blowing,
the garbage lids flying like frisbees and either
the roof's sprung a leak, or you left the tap running.
The paper's still empty, the poem unwritten.
You would have done better to have talked to your mother.
You miss it, it misses you. You miss each other.

2007

Paradise

Not many behold God
He is only for those of 100% pneuma
the rest listen to communiqués about miracles and floods
some day God will be seen by all

Report from Paradise, ZBIGNIEW HERBERT

Paradise is really the same as Britain
There's the class system for instance
Some only just scraped in
through the celestial portals
Was it something about the accent
the diphthongs perhaps or vowels
the cut of the jib or jacket
not quite *quite*
Even though they are good
not many behold God

For God cannot hobnob
with any old Tom, Dick or Harry, God cannot
be expected to pass the time
(He has none to waste
what with the heavenly choirs to hear, the wings to evaluate)
for each and every newcomer
much as He might wish
Just where does He draw the line
anyway? according to rumour
He is only for those of 100% pneuma

while those of 90%
check their barometers daily
hypochondriacs of the soul
eager (so near!) to be nearer
while the 99-percenters
are you might say the bluebloods
and if not aristocrats at the very least 'county'
and soon to be elevated
from the could-bes to the shoulds
The rest listen to communiqués about miracles and floods

and are content for the moment
to be there, to have made it
for after all, the options –
not exactly a Sunday school picnic –
are Purgatory like a negative not yet printed
or the famous flames of Hell
So they are patiently happy just to have been accepted
and though there is no date yet,
and when, no one can tell,
some day God will be seen by all

2007

Cullen in the Afterlife

He found it strange at first. A new dimension.
One he had never guessed. The fourth? The fifth?
How could he tell, who'd only known the third?
Something to do with eyesight, depth of field.
Perspective quite beyond him. Everything flat
or nearly flat. The vanishing point
they'd tried to teach at school, was out of sight
and out of mind. A blank.

Now, this diaphanous dimension – one
with neither up nor down, nor east nor west,
nor orienting star to give him north.
Even his name had left him. Strayed like a dog.
Yet he was bathed in some unearthly light,
a delicate no-colour that made his flesh
transparent, see-through, a Saran-wrap self.
His body without substance and his mind
with nothing to think about – although intact –
was totally minus purpose. He must *think*.

Think of a Rubens, he said to himself. But where
Rubens had been there was a void, a vast
emptiness – no opulence. And then
Cézanne who broke all matter up –
made light of it, in fact. And mad Van Gogh
who, blinded by the light, cut off his ear.
Gone – that shadowy assembly – vanished, done.
Gone without substance. Like himself. A shell.
Insensate in a flash. (What was that flash –
bereft of all but essence?) Was it death?
He wondered about the word, so filled with breath
yet breathless, breathless, breathless. A full stop.

'Divino Espirito Santo', he had said
once in Brazil, 'Soul of my very soul'.

He'd prayed in Portuguese, an easier tongue
for newly agnostic Anglos than his own,
burdened with shibboleths and past beliefs.
'Alma de minha alma' – liquid words
that made a calm within him. Where within?
Was there a word for it? Was it his heart?

Engulfed by love. Held in a healing beam
of love-light. Had he earned such love?
And how partake of such a gift when he
was handicapped by earthshine – wore the stars,
badges and medals of privilege and success?
De-sensitizers, brutalizers – all
the tricks that mammon plays to make one sleep.

He must wake up. He must expose and strip
successive layers to find his soul again.
Where had the rubble come from? He was like
a junk yard – cluttered, filled with scrap iron, tin.
As dead as any metal not in use.

So he must start once more. He had begun
how many times? Faint glimmerings and dim
memories of pasts behind the past
recently lived – the animal pasts and vague
vegetable pasts – those climbing vines and fruits;
and mineral pasts (a slower pulse) the shine
of gold and silver and the grey of iron.
The 'upward anguish'.
                    What a rush of wings
above him as he thought the phrase and knew
angels were overhead, and over them
a million suns and moons.

2009

Explanatory Notes

Ecce Homo

• In 1935, Page, who was spending the year in London, visited the Leicester Galleries with an older woman, a friend of a former teacher in Calgary. There they saw a sculpture of Christ by the American-born British sculptor, Jacob Epstein, entitled *Ecce Homo* ('Behold the man' [John 19:5]). Epstein's sculpture, *Rima*, depicts the jungle-girl heroine of *Green Mansions* by W. H. Hudson.

• Cronin ... *Hatter's Castle*: *Hatter's Castle* is a novel by A. J. Cronin.

Cullen

• April cruel ... 'April is the cruellest month' [T. S. Eliot, *The Waste Land*]

Puppets

• seaside Punch ... Pulcinella ... Bexhill ... Pepys: Punch and Judy shows were performed at seaside resorts such as Bexhill-on-Sea. The first record of a performance occurs in Samuel Pepys' diary. Punch is derived from the Neapolitan stock character Pulcinella.

Portrait of Marina

• dimity: 'a stout cotton fabric, woven with raised stripes or fancy figures' *[OED]*

Photos of a Salt Mine

• stope: 'a step-like working in the side of a pit' *[OED]*

• syncline: 'a line or axis towards which strata dip or slope down in opposite directions' *[OED]*

• anticline: 'a line or axis from which strata slope down or dip in opposite directions' *[OED]*

Images of Angels

• the nudes of Lawrence ... asexuality: The novelist D. H. Lawrence was also a painter whose erotic nudes were banned.

Arras

• Arras: 'a rich tapestry fabric, in which figures and scenes are woven in colours' *[OED]*

• espalier: 'a kind of lattice-work or frame-work of stakes upon which fruit trees or ornamental shrubs are trained' *[OED]*

• furl: 'to roll or gather up (a flag) into small compass' *[OED]*

• points a bone at me: 'aboriginal projective magic. A prepared human or kangaroo bone is pointed by a sorcerer at an intended victim (who may be miles away) to bring about his death' [note by Page]

This Frieze of Birds

• Dom. Robert: Guy de Chaunac Dom Robert, French priest and artist known for his intricate tapestry designs featuring birds

• wattle: 'mimosa' [note by Page]
• St. Francis ... brown robe: Saint Francis of Assisi, often depicted preaching to birds. Members of the Franciscan order typically wear brown habits.

Chimney Fire
• Rousseau the Douanier: Henri Julien Félix Rousseau, French primitive painter, known as 'Le Douanier' (the customs officer)

Giovanni and the Indians
• Giovanni: the Italian immigrant gardener for the Canadian embassy in Australia
• wattle: 'mimosa' [note by Page]

After Rain
• broderie anglaise: 'open embroidery on linen, cambric, etc.' [OED]
• Chantilly: 'applied to a delicate lace made originally at Chantilly, or to an article of apparel made of this lace' [OED]
• choux-fleurs: cauliflowers
• tulle: 'a fine silk bobbin-net used for women's dresses, veils, hats, etc.' [OED]

Bark Drawing
•Drawings by Australian aborigines made from natural pigments applied to strips of eucalyptus bark that have been flattened, dried and smoothed
• goanna: 'a large lizard' [note by Page]
• intaglio: 'a figure or design incised or engraved; a cutting or engraving in stone or other hard material' [OED]
• isinglass: 'a firm whitish semitransparent substance ... obtained from the ... air-bladders of some fresh-water fishes' [OED]
• bull roarer: 'a thin blade of wood which makes a loud thrumming sound when whirled on a cord. Its use in aborigine ceremonies warns off women and the uninitiated' [note by Page].
• dillybag: 'shopping bag; originally an aborigine's bag in which tribal treasures were kept' [note by Page]

Cook's Mountains
• The Glass Mountains are a series of steep-sided volcanic plugs which were named by Captain James Cook, who was reminded by their shape of the glassmaking furnaces, known as glasshouses, of his native Yorkshire.

Knitters
• Moore: Henry Moore, British sculptor
• Theseus ... maze ... daedal ... Minotaur: Theseus slew the Minotaur, half man half bull, in the maze built by Daedalus to contain it.

Brazilian House
• Ricardo: the gardener at the Canadian Embassy in Brazil

This Whole Green World

• Manuel: Manuel was Ricardo's assistant (see above).

• chrysoprase: 'the ancient name of a golden-green precious stone' *[OED]*

Natural History Museum

• baleen: 'a whale. *Obs.*' *[OED]*

• union-suit: 'a one-piece under-garment reaching to the ankles' *[OED]*

Brazilian Fazenda

• Fazenda: 'an estate or large farm. Also the home-stead belonging thereto' *[OED]*

• bridal hammock: 'wedding hammock. In Brazil they were double ... and white and elaborately tasselled' [e-mail from Page].

• Nossa Senhora ... Bahía: 'The large, carved Nossa Senhora ... was ... barefoot ... . I don't know why I said she had walked all the way from Bahía. Possibly for alliterative purposes' [e-mail from Page].

Cry Ararat!

• Ararat: the location of the mountain upon which Noah's ark came to rest after the Flood [Genesis 8:4]

Dark Kingdom

• Chalice ... Goat ... Sceptered Unicorn ... Crowned Hermaphrodite: alchemical symbols discussed in C.G. Jung's *Alchemical Studies* (Bollingen, 1967).

Travellers' Palm

• The sheaths of the stems of the travellers' palm hold rainwater, which can be used as an emergency drinking supply.

Three Gold Fish

• burning like Blake's *Tyger*: 'Tyger! Tyger! burning bright' [William Blake]

Leather Jacket

• Suhrawardi: Persian mystic theologian and philosopher. The quotation is from Farid al-Din Attar *Muslim Saints and Mystics Episodes from the Tadhkirat al-Auliya' (Memorial of the Saints)*, translated by A.J. Arberry (Routledge & Kegan Paul, 1966): xxiii.

Spinning

• tesseract ... sphered sphere: 'four-dimensional hypercube' *[OED]* and, by analogy, a four-dimensional sphere

Shaman

• *Diphyllodes magnificus:* a tropical bird found in New Guinea

Finches Feeding

• *sumi:* 'Japanese ink or blacking, composed of a mixture of carbon and glue molded into sticks or cakes. When rubbed into water on an inkstone, it becomes the common medium of the painter and writer.' *[OED]*

Macumba: Brazil

• Macumba: 'an Afro-Brazilian folk religion or cult combining elements of Brazilian Roman Catholicism and spiritualism with traditional African religious practices' *[OED]*. The poem describes the Macumba New Year's ceremony on Copacabana beach in Rio de Janeiro.

• *copa:* breakfast room

• changing the salt: salt was used to absorb excess humidity and had to be changed frequently

• *feijão:* bean

• Iemanjá: goddess of the ocean and of motherhood in Macumba

Seraphim

• Girasole: 'a sunflower. *Obs. rare*' *[OED]*

The Flower Bed

• the Omega point: 'a hypothesized end to evolutionary development in which all sentient life will converge into a supreme consciousness' *[OED]*

After Reading *Albino Pheasants* by Patrick Lane

• Patrick Lane: Canadian poet

• Barra de Navidad: ('Christmas sandbar'), a beach in Mexico where Page and her husband spent one Christmas [interview with Sandra Djwa].

Message

• 'It would be absurd to attempt to convey the meaning of Sufi thought and action in a conventional simplified or conversational manner. ... This absurdity is summarized by the Sufi tag as "sending a kiss by messenger"' [Idries Shah, *The Sufis* (Anchor Books, 1971): 20–21].

George Johnston Reading

• George Johnston: Canadian poet and translator

• your hives: Johnston kept bees.

• saga of heroic Gisli: The saga of Gisli recounts the story of Gisli who is outlawed because of a revenge killing he has committed. Johnston translated this as *The Saga of Gisli* (Dent, 1973).

• Gisli, crow-feeder: Gisli left his slain enemies as carrion for crows

• whey-Thorbjorn: Thorbjorn, father of Gisli, is attacked by his enemies who set his house on fire. He douses the fire with goatskins dipped in whey, and thereafter is known as whey-Thorbjorn.

• skaldic verse forms: 'Each stanza has eight lines – four pairs of lines; three stressed syllables per line, the third always trochaic. The paired lines are linked by alliteration. There is a half-rhyme in the first line of each pair, a full rhyme in the second.' [Page, *The Filled Pen*: 71].

- court metre: the most common skaldic metre
- Scarlatti: Giuseppe Domenico Scarlatti, Italian baroque keyboard composer.

Out Here: Flowering

- Jonathan Griffin: British poet. The quotation is from his poem 'Out There'.

Ours

- Patrick Anderson: English-born Canadian poet. He was one of the founders of *Preview*, with which Page was closely associated.

Deaf Mute in the Pear Tree

- Generalić. Primitive: Ivan Generalić, a Croatian primitive painter

Invisible Presences Fill the Air

- Anael, Phorlakh, Nisroc, Heiglot, Zlar: angels, representing, respectively, sexuality, the earth, freedom, snowstorms [Gustav Davidson, *A Dictionary of Angels, Including the Fallen Angels* (Free Press, 1967)]

Suffering

- Gurdjieff: George Ivanovich Gurdjieff, Russian spiritual teacher. The quotation is from *In Search of the Miraculous: Fragments of an Unknown Teaching*, by P.D. Ouspensky (Harcourt, Brace & World, 1949): 274.

Kaleidoscope

- John Murray: Byron's publisher.
- Quite a celestial kaleidoscope: *Don Juan*, 2.93.8
- Guiccioli: Teresa, Contessa Guiccioli, Byron's mistress
- *peau de soie*: 'a soft heavy silk, closely woven and with a dull satin face on both sides' *[OED]*
- Gwendolyn: Gwendolyn MacEwen, Canadian poet
your garden of square roots: 'The Garden of Square Roots: An Autobiography'

Lily on the Patio

- neutrino: 'each of three stable, uncharged leptons ..., associated respectively with the electron, the muon, and the tau lepton, which have very little mass and an extremely low probability of interaction with matter' *[OED]*

This Heavy Craft

- Icarus: Attempting to escape from Crete with wings created by his father Daedalus, Icarus flew too close to the sun and fell to his death when the wax attaching his wings melted.

Conversation

- This poem describes the collaboration between Page and Arie Aroch, Israeli painter and ambassador to Brazil, which resulted in the painting *Insects*.
- Corcovado: a mountain in Rio de Janeiro, known for the statue of Jesus on its peak

• additive colour: Additive colours are produced by adding the primary colours to one another in various proportions, as they are emitted directly from a source

Address at Simon Fraser

• the force that through the green fuse drives the flower: Dylan Thomas, 'The Force that through the Green Fuse Drives the Flower'

• can rap and knock and enter in our souls: Robert Browning, 'Bishop Blougram's Apology'

• had we but world enough and time: Andrew Marvell, 'To His Coy Mistress'

• the face (we) had/before the world was made: William Butler Yeats, 'Before the World Was Made'

• humanunkind … cummings: e.e. cummings, 'pity this busy monster, manunkind'

• Imagination is the star in man: cited by Jung in *Collected Works of C. G. Jung*, Vol. 12. 2nd ed. (Princeton UP, 1968): 277

• archaic torso of Apollo … Rilke, 'You must change your life': Rainer Maria Rilke, 'Archaic Torso of Apollo'

Love's Pavilion

• the Paraclete: 'a title given to the Holy Spirit (or occas. Christ): an advocate, intercessor; a helper or comforter' *[OED]*

• the Lord of the Dance: title of a hymn, words by Sydney Carter; may also refer to Nataraja, the depiction of the god Shiva as the cosmic dancer

• we shall dance and we shall sing: 'We must laugh and we must sing' [William Butler Yeats, 'A Dialogue of Self and Soul']

Planet Earth

• goffer: 'to make wavy by means of heated goffering-irons; to flute or crimp (the edge of lace, a frill, or trimming of any kind)' *[OED]*

Presences

• Aten … Nefertiti … Aknaten: Akhnaten (usual spelling) was a pharaoh who abandoned polytheism for a form of monotheism centring on the sun god Aten. Nefertiti was his wife.

The Gold Sun

• Phaeton: son of Helios, the sun god, received permission from his father to drive the chariot of the sun but lost control of it and caused great damage to the earth. Zeus killed him with a bolt of lightning to prevent further damage.

• Phoebus: 'the shining one', used of Apollo or of the sun god Helios

Poor Bird

• Seurat (pointilliste): Pointillisme is 'a technique of painting using tiny dots of various pure colours, which when viewed from a distance are blended by the viewer's eye. This technique was developed particularly by French neo-impressionist painters, notably Georges Seurat' [OED].

Hologram
• Kafka's castle: Franz Kafka, *The Castle*
• Escher: Maurits Cornelis Escher, Dutch graphic artist whose works often present impossible constructions
• Jurassic: 'applied to … the period between the Triassic and the Cretaceous' [OED], from about 200 to 145 million years ago

The Hidden Room
• Bodleian: the Oxford University Library
• Borges' aleph: In 'The Aleph' by Jorge Luis Borges, the Aleph is the point that contains all other points.
• magic square: 'a square array of numbers with the property that the sum of the numbers in each vertical, horizontal, or diagonal row is the same' [OED]

Like a Cruise Ship
• *biot:* a dimensionless number used in heat transfer calculations, named after the French physicist Jean-Baptiste Biot
• *quark:* 'each of a group of subatomic particles regarded (with leptons) as basic constituents of matter, and postulated never to occur in the free state' [OED]
• *nanosecond:* 'one thousand-millionth of a second' [OED]

But We Rhyme in Heaven
• Dorothy Livesay: Canadian poet

Alphabetical
• xx, xy: In most mammals, females have two of the same kind of sex chromosome (XX), and males have two distinct sex chromosomes (XY).
• de Bono's … *po*: term coined by Edward de Bono, for an idea which encourages lateral thinking
• gift from Arabia: The concept of zero was transmitted by the Arabs to the West from Hindu mathematics.

Cosmologies
• tao: 'in Taoism, an absolute entity which is the source of the universe; the way in which this absolute entity functions' [OED]

Even Lucifer
• a good man: Page's recently deceased husband, William Arthur Irwin

Poem Canzonic with love to AMK
• AMK is the Canadian poet, Abraham Moses Klein, whom Page first met through *Preview* magazine. 'Canzonic' is from 'canzone': 'a song, a ballad; a species of lyric,

closely resembling the madrigal but less strict in style' *[OED]*.

• *ultramar:* ultramarine, from the Portuguese *ultramar azul*

• arcanum: 'one of the supposed great secrets of nature which the alchemists aimed at discovering' *[OED]*

• Om: 'a sacred syllable or invocation traditionally uttered at the beginning and end of prayer and meditation' *[OED]*

• St. Elmo's fire: 'the ball of light which is sometimes seen on a ship (esp. about the masts or yard-arms) during a storm' *[OED]*

Ah, by the Golden Lilies

• *sambas jocosos:* playful sambas

• *macumba:* 'an Afro-Brazilian folk religion or cult combining elements of Brazilian Roman Catholicism and spiritualism with traditional African religious practices' *[OED]*

• *feijoada:* a stew of beans, beef and pork, popular in Brazil

• Bahían *vatapá:* a dish made from bread, shrimp, coconut milk and palm oil mashed into a creamy paste, popular in the Brazilian state of Bahía

The Blue Guitar

• tell it slant … Emily: Emily Dickinson, 'Tell all the Truth But Tell It Slant'

Green, How Much I Want You Green

• Pleistocene: 'the earliest epoch of the Quaternary period, between about 1,640,000 and 10,000 years ago'

• Snow Queen: the queen of the snowflakes in 'The Snow Queen' by Hans Christian Andersen

Coal and Roses – A Triple Glosa

• Perseid: 'an annual shower of meteors which appear to radiate from the constellation Perseus during late July and August' *[OED]*

• Pleiades: 'prominent open cluster of stars in the constellation Taurus' *[OED]*

Your Slightest Look

• Morpheus: 'the god of dreams (popularly often taken as the god of sleep), used *allusively* with reference to his ability to induce dreams or sleep. Hence also (as a personification): sleep; a soporific substance, etc.' *[OED]*

Cullen in the Afterlife

• Alma de minha alma: 'soul of my soul,' from a prayer to the Holy Ghost ('Divino Espirito Santo') which Page learned in Brazil

• earthshine: 'the partial illumination of the dark portion of the moon's surface by light reflected from the earth' *[OED]*

• upward anguish: Humbert Wolfe, *The Upward Anguish*

Title Index

Index of First Lines

About P. K. Page

P. K. Page was born November 23, 1916, at Swanage, Dorset, England and died January 14, 2010, at Victoria, British Columbia, Canada. In 1919 she left England with her family and settled in Red Deer, Alberta. She went to school in Calgary and Winnipeg and in the early 1940s moved to Montreal where she worked as a filing clerk and researcher. She belonged to a group that founded the magazine *Preview* (1942–45) and was associated with F. R. Scott, Patrick Anderson, Bruce Ruddick, Neufville Shaw and A. M. Klein. Her first book published was *Unit of Five* (1944), where her poetry appeared alongside that of Louis Dudek and Raymond Souster. From 1946 to 1950 Page worked for the National Film Board as a scriptwriter. In 1950 she married William Arthur Irwin and later studied art in Brazil, Mexico and New York.

P. K. Page is the author of dozens of books, including poetry, a novel, short stories, essays and books for children. A memoir entitled *Brazilian Journal* is based on her extended stay in Brazil with her husband who served as the Canadian Ambassador there from 1957 to 1959. A memoir in verse, *Hand Luggage*, explores in a poetic voice Page's life in the arts and in the world.

Awarded a Governor General's Award for poetry *(The Metal and the Flower)* in 1954, Page was also on the short list for the Griffin Prize for Poetry *(Planet Earth)* in 2003 and, posthumously, in 2010 *(Coal and Roses),* and she was awarded the BC Lieutenant Governor's Award for Literary Excellence in 2004. She had numerous honorary degrees, received the Order of British Columbia and was a Fellow of the Royal Society of Canada. She was also appointed a Companion of the Order of Canada.

Painting under the name of P. K. Irwin she mounted one-woman shows in Mexico and Canada and exhibited in various group shows. Her work is represented in the permanent collections of the National Gallery of Canada, the Art Gallery of Ontario, the Victoria Art Gallery and many other collections here and abroad.